Second Edition

# Effective Program Evaluation

MARDALE DUNSWORTH

DAWN BILLINGS

A Joint Publication

Solution Tree

naesp

555 North Morton Street
Bloomington, IN 47404
800.733.6786 (toll free) / 812.336.7700
FAX: 812.336.7790

email: info@solution-tree.com
solution-tree.com

Visit **go.solution-tree.com/schoolimprovement** to download the reproducibles in this book.

Printed in the United States of America

15 14 13 12 11     1 2 3 4 5

Library of Congress Cataloging-in-Publication Data

Dunsworth, Mardale.
  Effective program evaluation / Mardale Dunsworth, Dawn Billings. -- 2nd ed.
      p. cm.
  Includes bibliographical references and index.
  ISBN 978-1-935542-90-2 (perfect bound) -- ISBN 978-1-935542-91-9 (library edition)
1.  School improvement programs--United States. 2.  Academic achievement--United States. 3.  Educational indicators.  I. Billings, Dawn L. II. Dunsworth, Mardale High-performing school. III. Title.
  LB2822.82.D86 2012
  371.2'07--dc23
                    2011020380

**Solution Tree**
Jeffrey C. Jones, CEO & President

**Solution Tree Press**
*President:* Douglas M. Rife
*Publisher:* Robert D. Clouse
*Vice President of Production:* Gretchen Knapp
*Managing Production Editor:* Caroline Wise
*Copy Editors:* David Eisnitz
                        Tara Perkins
*Proofreader:* Sarah Payne-Mills
*Text Designer:* Jenn Taylor
*Cover Designer:* Orlando Angel

# ACKNOWLEDGMENTS

Solution Tree Press would like to thank the following reviewers:

Cindy DeClercq
Executive Director, Learning Support Services
Poway Unified School District
San Diego, California

Cynthia De La Garza
Principal
Charles Graebner Elementary School
San Antonio, Texas

Gabriel Duran
Principal
Pacific Boulevard School
Huntington Park, California

Trudy Grafton
Principal
Study Elementary School
Fort Wayne, Indiana

Ken Gregorich
Retired Elementary Principal
Yakima, Washington

Bonnie K. Knowlan
Principal
South Elementary
Jackson, Missouri

Holly Williams
Director, Department of Program Evaluation
Austin Independent School District
Austin, Texas

Visit **go.solution-tree.com/schoolimprovement**
to download the reproducibles in this book.

# TABLE OF CONTENTS

*Reproducible pages are in italics.*

**3**  Gathering Data

**4**  Analyzing the Data

# ABOUT THE AUTHORS

**Mardale Dunsworth** served as the director of professional development for the Office of Superintendent of Public Instruction in Washington State. Ms. Dunsworth led the design and development of an innovative technology-enhanced statewide professional development and certification system including the design and creation of an online licensing process, an events registration site, and a centralized registry for high-quality professional development connecting school improvement planning and professional growth planning for teachers.

As the director of curriculum, instruction, and professional technical education at the Oregon Department of Education, Ms. Dunsworth administered federal grant programs and designed and managed the state's assistance program to low-achieving schools.

Ms. Dunsworth's legislative experience includes her work as the legislative liaison to the Senate and House Education Committees. She holds a bachelor's degree in public policy and administration and a master's degree in education (curriculum and instruction).

**Dawn Billings** served as assistant superintendent of public instruction for the state of Washington. Ms. Billings led the design and development of Washington State Professional Development Standards that provided the research base for Washington's school and district efforts in professional development. She was responsible for providing statewide professional development for administrators and teachers, including research-based professional development institutes attended by more than 9,000 educators annually.

As the director of curriculum and instruction for the Oregon Department of Education, Ms. Billings led the design of services to low-achieving schools, the development of the grade-level standards in English and language arts, math, science, social studies, the arts, physical education, and foreign languages. She was the co-author of Oregon's Reading First grant program and the state charter schools program.

Ms. Billings has taught middle and high schools in urban and rural school districts and held a variety of administrative positions in public education and business and industry. She has a bachelor's degree in education (history), and a master's degree in secondary education.

Mardale Dunsworth and Dawn Billings founded School Synergy in 2005. Strong advocates for the use of a rich mix of survey, interview, observational, student learning, and achievement data for decision making, Ms. Dunsworth and Ms. Billings are coauthors of *The High-Performing School: Benchmarking the 10 Indicators of Effectiveness,* a *ForeWord* magazine Book of the Year finalist. Among its other projects, School Synergy was selected as a turnaround partner by one of the Race to the Top states, where it is working to provide the research-based evaluation processes, strategic interventions, and ongoing progress-monitoring system in which student learning is accelerated and the learning environment supports students, staff, and families.

To learn more about the authors' work, visit www.schoolsynergy.org.

To book Mardale Dunsworth or Dawn Billings for professional development, contact pd@solution-tree.com.

# INTRODUCTION

It can be surprisingly difficult to ensure that the decisions you make as a school principal are the correct ones, especially when expert or staff opinion is conflicting, research results are mixed, or there is a lack of or confusing data on which to base those decisions. This is exactly the problem that program evaluation is designed to solve. It provides a logical and evidence-based method to make decisions about complex or controversial issues.

Program evaluation is a systematic way to compare the current performance of a program, practice, or strategy to the outcomes that were anticipated when the program was implemented. It provides a robust view of existing practices, and it objectively displays what is working well, what could be improved, and how those improvements could be made. Because the evaluation process described here is transparent, it also helps build the school and community support necessary to implement the recommended changes that grow from the evaluation.

Principals are, at the end of the day, responsible for ensuring that the instructional program meets the needs of all students, and that school goals are achieved. Principals play a key role in overseeing this process and creating a shared commitment to both the evaluation and in implementing the recommendations that emerge.

This *Essentials for Principals* guide walks school leaders step by step through the program evaluation cycle and provides principals with the tools and processes needed to conduct a successful evaluation. The appendix, The Vocabulary of Program Evaluation (page 67), provides a quick reference glossary of important terms you will encounter throughout this guide. Discussing this glossary with the evaluation team will ensure that everyone working on the evaluation shares a common understanding when using these terms.

We know that you will find program evaluation to be a valuable tool in meeting the needs of your school and community. Program evaluation is steeped in effective schools research, the process is straightforward, and the results are powerful.

# 1

# Defining Program Evaluation

As legislation and departments of education place increasing emphasis on performance and accountability, school leaders are more frequently called on to make decisions about the effectiveness of school programs, practices, and strategies. How good those decisions turn out to be is largely a function of the quality of information on which the decision was based. Program evaluation provides school leaders with the information they need to make good decisions about programs, practices, and strategies in use or being considered for use at a school or district. It can answer questions such as:

- How effective is our math program?

- How effective is our reading intervention program?

- How well does our classroom instruction align with our curriculum and learning goals?

- Are our response to intervention (RTI) strategies meeting the needs of all students?

- To what degree are we focusing on higher-order thinking skills?

- How effective is our family and community involvement program?

- Are our grouping and regrouping practices effective and efficient?

- How effective is our school behavior program?

As in these examples, the specific questions addressed by the evaluation process will vary, but the process used to find the answers will be similar. The goal of program evaluation is to use data to guide decisions about how well school programs are working and to do so in a way that is both time and cost effective.

## Why Conduct a Program Evaluation?

Program evaluation is an essential tool in many professions, including medicine, science, government, engineering, and business. Learning how to conduct an evaluation enables leaders "to create the best possible programs, to learn from mistakes, to make modifications as needed, to monitor progress toward program goals, and to judge the success of the program in achieving its short-term, intermediate, and long-term outcomes" (Centers for Disease Control and Prevention, 2005, p. 5). Evaluation can be used to assess key aspects of a program's progress and implementation, and it can provide vital data to inform next steps. It can:

- Determine the extent to which a program is meeting its goals

- Measure consistency of program delivery

- Determine whether to continue, modify, or abandon an existing program

- Address conflicting opinions about an existing program, practice, or strategy

## Determine the Extent to Which a Program Is Meeting Its Goals

Is the program, practice, or strategy meeting the goals expected of it when it was selected? Is it serving its purpose now? Is it working equally well for all students, or are some groups of students (for example, academically struggling students, special education students, or English learners) benefiting more or less from the program? In looking at the effectiveness of a math program, for example, the evaluation might measure the program's impact on students from various racial and ethnic groups, different grade levels, or in different classrooms.

## Measure Consistency of Program Delivery

Also known as *fidelity of implementation,* this is the degree to which the activities and methods used in the program are consistent with the way they were intended to be used by the program authors or creators (Century, Freeman, & Rudnick, 2008). It includes answers to questions such as (O'Connell, 2007):

- To what degree do the instructional strategies and delivery methods used at the school match those recommended in the program design?

- Does implementation vary from classroom to classroom?

- Do the time and frequency of instruction match that recommended in the program design?

- How well does the instructional setting (for example, general classroom, small-group intervention, or after-school or summer program) match the program's recommended instructional setting?

- Does the target population indicated in the program design match the population participating in the program at the school site?

- How closely do the quality and duration of professional development in the program match what is recommended by the program authors?

## Determine Whether to Continue, Modify, or Abandon an Existing Program

Programs are a coordinated set of strategies and practices that address a common goal, such as student mastery of math standards. Programs can range from textbook series to discipline systems, from dropout prevention programs to academic intervention programs. Here the evaluation can provide the information needed by a school leader to determine whether a specific program is meeting the needs of the school, students, or the community and what the next course of action should be.

## Address Conflicting Opinions About an Existing Program, Practice, or Strategy

If some staff, parents, or students believe the program, practice, or strategy has problems, what is the nature of those problems, and what are some possible solutions? For example, if some teachers are highly satisfied with the math program while others have negative opinions, a well-designed program evaluation can identify the source of these differing opinions and develop recommendations to gain consensus. Perhaps the teachers who are more positive about the program received better training in the use of the program, in which case professional development may be the answer, or perhaps the program is more successful with some students than with others, in which case the program may need to be more clearly targeted at a specific group of students.

# The Role of the Principal in Program Evaluation

The principal plays a pivotal role in overseeing the evaluation process, creating a shared commitment to conducting an effective evaluation, and making decisions based on the evaluation team's recommendations. While many responsibilities can be delegated to a committed evaluation team, in successful evaluations, the principal takes responsibility for the following (Mid-continent Research for Education and Learning [McREL], 2000):

- Helping teachers, parents, students, staff, and other stakeholders gain a common understanding of the purposes and value of the evaluation

- Setting up a team to design and carry out the evaluation

- Providing release time as needed for the team to do its work

- Stressing the importance of setting program goals and objectives that are tied to students' academic performance

- Ensuring that goals are specific enough to provide direction, yet general enough to allow flexibility in implementation

- Promoting program evaluation as one of many aspects of school improvement and strategic planning

- Dispelling fears that the evaluation will be used to assign blame

- Clarifying expectations about the evaluation process with teachers, parents, service providers, and other key stakeholders

- Helping create an environment of reflective inquiry and improvement by asking questions about evidence of student learning

- Encouraging staff members to use data by giving them time and opportunities to gather and analyze data and report findings

- Seeking additional resources for evaluation as needed

- Regularly reporting progress to stakeholders, which will build support for the effort, particularly if incremental improvements can be demonstrated

- Helping stakeholders understand that improvement is not always a smooth process and that it occurs over time

# The Steps of Program Evaluation

While many school improvement strategies are complex and multifaceted, program evaluation is a straightforward five-step process when designed and carried out as described in the following chapters:

1. Creating and completing a program evaluation blueprint to define the purpose and scope of the evaluation

2. Gathering data needed to assess a program's effectiveness

3. Analyzing the data in order to identify a program's strengths and weaknesses

4. Using the results of the program evaluation to plan next steps

5. Communicating results to stakeholders in order to build community involvement and support

In addition to the discussion of each step in the following chapters, the appendix (page 67) contains valuable notes on core terminology and concepts essential to program evaluation.

CHAPTER 2

# Creating and Completing a Program Evaluation Blueprint

A tool that will be helpful in planning for and carrying out your program evaluation is the program evaluation blueprint. The blueprint identifies the:

1. Purpose of the evaluation

2. Evaluation team members

3. Research questions

4. Data collection methods

5. Timelines

6. Team members' responsibilities

7. Resources needed to complete the evaluation

In addition to being helpful in planning the evaluation, the blueprint is also useful in communicating about the evaluation. Questions about the evaluation can often be answered by simply providing a completed copy of the blueprint.

The blueprint will also help those responsible for implementing the evaluation resist *scope creep*—the expansion of a project's breadth or depth beyond its original objectives. At some point in the evaluation, an evaluation team may be tempted to "improve" on the existing plan by adding new questions, grade levels, or data collections. Sticking to the plan outlined in the blueprint will help prevent the plan from becoming too large or too complex. Figure 2.1 (page 8) shows the template.

As we move through a description of each step of the evaluation in this chapter, we will illustrate how that step would appear in an example blueprint.

| Define Purpose | Select Program Evaluation Team | Determine Program Evaluation Research Questions | Identify Data Collection Methods | Establish Timelines | Assign Responsibilities | Identify Resources |
|---|---|---|---|---|---|---|
|  |  |  |  |  |  |  |

Figure 2.1: The program evaluation blueprint.

# Defining Purpose

The first step in a program evaluation is crafting a statement that defines the purpose of the evaluation. This purpose statement will make it much easier to develop the evaluation plan and gather appropriate evidence to support the decision making that will follow the evaluation.

Begin by clearly defining the program that will be the subject of the evaluation. This sets the parameters of the evaluation. The program definition contains the description of the program, practice, or strategy that will be examined and, when appropriate, the grade levels at which the examination will occur. Some examples of programs are grades K–3 math, student engagement in grades 9–12, classroom management strategies in grades 4–8, and practices to increase school attendance rates at grade 9. In a program definition of K–3 math, it is clear that the evaluation will not be examining curricular areas outside of math nor grade levels below or above K–3.

Next, merge the program definition with a statement that explains the overarching purpose of the program evaluation. This statement can be phrased as simply as some of the following examples:

- The purpose of this program evaluation is to determine the degree to which our K–3 math program is resulting in students entering grade 4 math at grade level.

- The purpose of this program evaluation is to determine the degree to which the K–6 math curriculum has attained full alignment to state or Common Core math standards.

- The purpose of this evaluation is to determine the degree to which our recently adopted math intervention program has helped close achievement gaps in grades 3 through 5.

- The purpose of this program evaluation is to determine the degree to which the new classroom management program has resulted in fewer disciplinary actions schoolwide.

- The purpose of this evaluation is to determine the degree to which the current attendance policies and practices have improved student attendance schoolwide.

Although identifying a program evaluation's purpose may seem like the easiest part of the process, it is important to give serious thought to this step. An ill-defined purpose can result in off-target data collection or ambiguous findings that do not provide the proper information needed for decision making. A statement that is too narrowly defined may lead to results that are meaningless. Think about program evaluation in broad terms, and focus and narrow the questions as you continue planning.

When the purpose statement has been agreed upon, enter it into the first column of the blueprint as shown in figure 2.2 (page 10).

| Define Purpose | Select Program Evaluation Team | Determine Program Evaluation Research Questions | Identify Data Collection Methods | Establish Timelines | Assign Responsibilities | Identify Resources |
|---|---|---|---|---|---|---|
| The purpose of this program evaluation is to determine the degree to which our K–3 math program is resulting in students entering grade 4 math at grade level. | | | | | | |

Figure 2.2: Sample evaluation blueprint.

# Selecting the Program Evaluation Team

The work of the program evaluation needs to be a shared responsibility. Under the principal's leadership, a program evaluation team will carry out the work of the evaluation. Ideally, team membership will include classroom teachers, specialists, and other informed stakeholders. The program evaluation team needs to be small enough to be nimble and communicate easily and large enough to ensure the work gets done well and on time. This usually means about five to seven people, plus the principal.

The members should bring a mix of skills, interests, and experience to the evaluation team. Members of the program evaluation team should:

- Represent a variety of perspectives on the program being evaluated (they must also be willing to be impartial in their review)

- Be knowledgeable about the program, practice, or strategy being evaluated

- Be from a mix of grade levels and subjects, when applicable

- Have the ability to interview and capture responses accurately

- Be discreet and respect the confidentiality of interviews and team work sessions

- Have the ability to communicate results to other stakeholders by a variety of methods, including charts, graphs, and simple statistical displays (such as percentages and percentiles)

- Have the ability to put in some extra hours (for which they should be compensated)

- Be able to follow defined processes

- Produce high-quality products on time

- Have the respect of their colleagues

Under the direction of the principal, the evaluation team members will have primary responsibility for carrying out the evaluation and will make recommendations to the principal or administrative team upon completion of the program evaluation. In addition to individual strengths, skills, and knowledge, group dynamics will be important. As a group, the team will need to be able to work well together, resolve conflicts with respect, communicate effectively, and accomplish their tasks in a timely manner.

## Establish Group Norms

It may be a good idea to appoint an evaluation team leader or facilitator who can help the evaluation team stay on track in terms of group operating agreements, timelines, scope, and objectivity. An excellent way to avoid conflicts before they become problems is to ask the evaluation team to agree on team norms, such as those shown in figure 2.3 (page 12).

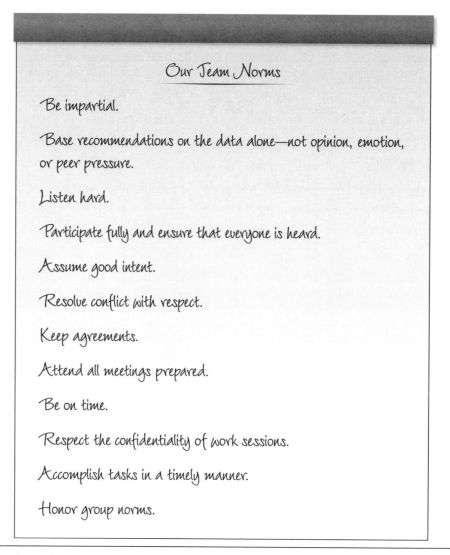

*Our Team Norms*

Be impartial.

Base recommendations on the data alone—not opinion, emotion, or peer pressure.

Listen hard.

Participate fully and ensure that everyone is heard.

Assume good intent.

Resolve conflict with respect.

Keep agreements.

Attend all meetings prepared.

Be on time.

Respect the confidentiality of work sessions.

Accomplish tasks in a timely manner.

Honor group norms.

Figure 2.3: Sample evaluation team norms.

## Communicate the Process Early

Talking with the staff about an upcoming program evaluation well before it begins will help alleviate concerns about the outcomes. Similarly, providing the opportunity for staff members to indicate interest in serving on the team will create greater interest and buy-in. Use the skills and abilities listed on page 11 to select team members. Let staff members know that you will be looking for a specific mix of skills and experience within the team, and that there may be more interest in serving than spaces available, so not everyone who volunteers may be selected. Stress that there will be opportunities to provide input during the evaluation process and that you welcome that involvement. Conversely, if there are fewer volunteers than necessary, think about those on staff who have the skills and abilities needed, and approach them directly.

Once the evaluation team has been selected, the second column of the evaluation blueprint can be completed, as shown in figure 2.4.

| Define Purpose | Select Program Evaluation Team | Determine Program Evaluation Research Questions | Identify Data Collection Methods | Establish Timelines | Assign Responsibilities | Identify Resources |
|---|---|---|---|---|---|---|
| The purpose of this program evaluation is to determine the degree to which our K–3 math program is resulting in students entering grade 4 math at grade level. | Principal: Jayne Tenn<br><br>Curriculum director: Jon Flint<br><br>Math coach: Judy Anderson<br><br>Grade-level chairs K–4:<br>  Steve Mille<br>  Nick Harnisch<br>  Sabrina Black<br>  Ashlee Grace<br>  Pam Oki | | | | | |

Figure 2.4: Sample evaluation blueprint, continued.

## Set a Communication Schedule

Once the purpose statement has been crafted and the team members selected, you are ready to convene the team to set up a communication schedule and to develop the research questions that will be the foundation of the program evaluation data collection. It works well to set up regular communication times with the team once or twice a week. For staff members, this works best just before or just after school. For other members who are not school staff and for whom these times may not be as convenient, arranging for access via technology works well.

At one of the first team meetings, members should collaboratively set the meeting schedule for the duration of the evaluation project. You can then add those dates to your calendar and let the team know at which meetings you will be present so that decisions requiring principal approval can be scheduled to take place during those meetings. As you and the team build the communications and task schedule, keep in mind that almost everyone working on the evaluation has other, more primary responsibilities. The evaluation will need to mesh with the normal flow of their work schedules.

# Determining Program Evaluation Research Questions

Next, it is time to introduce the team to the purpose statement and to begin brainstorming the research questions that will help the team answer the overarching question framed in the purpose statement. These questions need to be specific enough to be measured in the data collection and provide enough depth that the data collected will yield a full picture of the current state of the program, practice, or strategy.

Figure 2.5 shows a sample purpose statement and the questions that emerged from an evaluation team brainstorming session.

When the team has selected the questions and determined that there is a way to collect data to get at the answers, these are then added to the third column of the blueprint, as shown in figure 2.6 (page 16).

This is a good point for the principal to review the work so far to make sure it will supply the information needed to answer the purpose statement. If the research questions are not clear, or if the team is not meshing or lacks needed skills and abilities, go back and attend to those issues before moving on.

## Purpose Statement

The purpose of this program evaluation is to determine the degree to which our K–3 math program is resulting in students entering grade 4 math at grade level.

Program evaluation research questions:

What measures do we use to determine what students know and are able to do in math at the end of grades K, 1, 2, and 3?

What measures do we use to determine what students know and are able to do in math at the beginning of grade 4?

Do those measures align with state or Common Core math standards?

What do these measures tell us about the level of student knowledge and skills at each grade level?

What do those measures tell us about the level of student knowledge and skills at the beginning of grade 4?

How do students who have attended our school in all grades K–3 do on these measures compared to students who have attended our school for less time?

Are there differences in achievement between groups of students (for example, economically disadvantaged, English learners, special education)?

Is the curriculum aligned both vertically (grade to grade) and horizontally (among all classes at the same grade level)?

Does that curriculum match what is being taught in each classroom?

Does implementation of the curriculum vary in terms of time, materials, expectations, and pacing?

What instructional materials are we using?

Figure 2.5: Results of a research question brainstorming session.

| Define Purpose | Select Program Evaluation Team | Determine Program Evaluation Research Questions | Identify Data Collection Methods | Establish Timelines | Assign Responsibilities | Identify Resources |
|---|---|---|---|---|---|---|
| The purpose of this program evaluation is to determine the degree to which our K–3 math program is resulting in students entering grade 4 math at grade level. | Principal: Jayne Tenn<br><br>Curriculum director: Jon Flint<br><br>Math coach: Judy Anderson<br><br>Grade-level chairs K–4:<br>Steve Mille<br>Nick Harnisch<br>Sabrina Black<br>Ashlee Grace<br>Pam Oki | A. What measures do our teachers use to determine what students know and are able to do in math at the end of grades K, 1, 2, and 3?<br><br>B. What measures do we use to determine what students know and are able to do in math at the beginning of grade 4?<br><br>C. Do all of these measures align with state or Common Core standards in math? | | | | |

Figure 2.6: Sample evaluation blueprint, continued.

# Identifying Data Collection Methods

The way the data is collected depends on the research questions to be answered. In matching the data collection methods to the questions, there are four broad categories of data that schools most often use in program evaluations:

1. **Student learning data.** Includes summative and interim assessments, such as state test results, school or district assessments, end-of-course examinations, grade point averages, and on-time promotion rates

2. **Teacher data.** Includes data that describe staff characteristics, such as effectiveness measures, professional preparation, experience, attendance, and participation in individual, school, and district-level professional development

3. **Demographic data.** Includes descriptive information, such as student and teacher attendance rates, student socioeconomic status (that is, measures of poverty), gender, ethnicity, and other factors that describe the context in which the program operates

4. **Perception data.** Includes information related to what students, parents, teachers, and others think or believe about a program, practice, or strategy

Some of this information, such as statewide assessment results, will be readily at hand, or at least attainable via a review of school and district records. Other data will need to be collected through a variety of other methods that will be discussed in this section. Regardless of the source of the data, program evaluations should employ more than a single type of data in answering the research questions. This will provide multiple perspectives on which to base decision making. When considering which data would best be collected through which data source, be sure to consider those that may be of particular importance to a group of stakeholders, as its absence may weaken confidence in the results of the evaluation. To collect data in the areas described, six kinds of data collection tools are commonly used:

1. Surveys

2. Interviews

3. Focus groups

4. Classroom observations

5. Samples of student work

6. Documentary evidence

## Surveys

Surveys are typically used when information is desired from a relatively large number of respondents or if it would be logistically difficult to talk with the respondents face to face (for example, if you wanted to collect information from every parent at the school). Surveys are most effective when they protect the anonymity of the respondents. Most people will be frank and open only if they are not worried about repercussions resulting from their responses. Surveys may use either of the two following types of questions, or a combination of these.

## Close-Ended Questions

When a survey uses close-ended questions, respondents are provided with a list of options and asked to select answers from among these. Examples of close-ended survey questions include yes/no, true/false, multiple-choice questions, or Likert-scale classifications, such as those shown in figure 2.7.

Advantages of close-ended questions are that a large amount of data can be collected efficiently, and the responses can be readily converted into numbers for a statistical analysis. The disadvantages to close-ended questions are that response choices are limited to preselected answers, none of which may accurately reflect the respondent's opinion, and they do not allow the respondents to expand or explain their responses.

In the following example of a close-ended question from a survey of fifth- and sixth-grade students (fig. 2.7), we can see that the student in this survey believes the math class is not challenging. However, we cannot tell from the response why the student is not challenged, nor is there a way for the student to share his or her ideas on how to increase the challenge.

| | Strongly Agree ☺ | Agree | Not Sure | Disagree | Strongly Disagree ☹ | Not Applicable |
|---|---|---|---|---|---|---|
| My math class is challenging. | | | | ✔ | | |

Figure 2.7: Example of a close-ended survey item of a sixth-grade student.

## Open-Ended Questions

Open-ended questions are phrased so that respondents are encouraged to explain their answers and reactions to the question. Open-ended questions provide richer information, revealing beliefs, attitudes, and understandings of the subject that could not be captured in a close-ended survey. Open-ended questions allow the respondent to express new ideas that may not have been considered by the evaluation team. In addition, they ensure that respondents don't feel controlled or confined to a preselected set of responses. Two disadvantages to open-ended questions are that (1) fewer questions can be asked since written responses to each question will take the respondent longer to complete, and (2) results cannot be easily analyzed numerically. Figure 2.8 provides an example of an open-ended question.

What are three things your teacher could do to make learning math more interesting to you?

1. _____

2. _____

3. _____

Figure 2.8: Example of an open-ended survey question of a sixth-grade student.

# Interviews

Interviews are often used when the team requires more detailed perceptual information than a survey can provide, or when there are smaller groups of respondents. Although interviewing can be time consuming, it provides information that may not emerge from other methods. For many evaluations, it will not be necessary to interview every teacher in the school. For example, in an evaluation of the effectiveness of the K–3 math program, the evaluation team may decide to interview the school's K–3 teachers (including special education and English learner teachers), math coaches, and the district curriculum administrator to learn more about the strengths and weaknesses of the K–3 math program from their vantage points.

Although there are any number of ways an interview can be conducted, all interview questions should be open ended in order to draw out the most information. Open-ended questions can't be answered by a simple *yes* or *no*. Instead, the questions require the respondent to explain or give examples to support his or her responses. For example, ask, "How do you ensure that your math lessons are academically challenging for all students?" not, "Are your math classes academically challenging for all students?" If the team's set of interview questions can be answered with *yes* or *no*, either redraft them to make them open ended or consider including them in a survey rather than in an interview.

In a *preset interview*, the interviewer has a list of questions that are asked in a preset order: first question one, then question two, and so on. This type of interview is fairly simple to carry out and record, but the interview will have few conversational characteristics and may appear stilted as the questions do not expand upon the respondent's answers to the previous question.

In a *free-flowing interview*, the interviewer has a predetermined set of questions that must be asked, but there is no requirement that the questions be asked in a particular order. This interview model provides a more natural conversational flow while still obtaining the specific information required. While effective, it is more commonly used by interviewers who are more experienced in interviewing, as it requires practice to ensure that all questions are adequately addressed in the time allotted for the interview (W. K. Kellogg Foundation, 2004).

Interviews are particularly useful in soliciting information about key stakeholders' perceptions of the program. However, processing interview data may require extra time. Supplying interviewers with an electronic template from which they can read the questions, and on which they can record the responses, frees them from organizational work following the interview. Typing the responses directly onto the template as the interview is occurring will save a great deal of time later. If possible, use interviewers who can ask questions and type the responses as they go. If this is not feasible, each interviewer will need to be accompanied by a record keeper who will type in responses as the interview progresses.

When using interviewing as a data collection method, time must be allocated to train the interviewers. This training should address the importance of keeping interview responses confidential. Interviewees will also need to be assured that their responses will be anonymous and that their opinions will be respected. The training should also emphasize the importance of both asking every question in the interview and accurately recording responses without inserting personal bias.

## Focus Groups

Focus groups are structured interviews used to gather information from members of a clearly defined audience. Focus groups are effective tools "when the security of the group allows members who are lower in the 'power hierarchy' within an organization to express feelings and experiences that they would not otherwise share" (New York State Teacher Centers, 2008, p. 2). Examples of groups that may be good candidates for focus-group interviews include first-year teachers, parents, and educational assistants.

In those situations in which there is organizational conflict or in which certain groups feel alienated, focus groups are particularly valuable. In these cases, people may feel more listened to in a focus group, resulting in a more forthright exchange of information: "Because a group, rather than an individual, is asked to respond to questions, dialogue tends to take on a life of its own. Participants 'piggy-back' on the comments of others and add a richness to the dialogue that could not be achieved through a one-on-one interview" (Rennekamp & Nall, n.d., p. 1). As conversation unfolds, the information collected about the program may be both broader and deeper than that gained from a series of individual interviews.

Focus groups usually consist of between six and twelve participants, although they can be much larger and still work fairly well. Depending on the number of questions and size of the group, they typically last about sixty minutes, although they can be as short as forty-five minutes. The agenda should be limited to five or six questions so there is ample time for the group members to build on one another's ideas.

Unlike one-on-one interviews in which the pace of the interviews can be more easily controlled by the interviewer, focus groups are faster paced and usually require both an interviewer and a recorder. The interviewer asks the questions of the participants and balances the need to ensure that respondents have the opportunity to fully articulate their thoughts with the need to ensure that everyone is heard from in the time available. The recorder meanwhile records responses directly onto an electronic response template. Good times to schedule parent or community focus groups are just before and just after school or in the evening. If evening focus groups are scheduled, a light dinner and childcare are additional inducements to attend.

# Classroom Observations

Observing students and teachers in classrooms is most useful when the evaluation is focused on classroom-based programs, practices, or strategies, such as instructional methods, pacing, fidelity of implementation of a specific program or strategy, or classroom discipline.

School principals are often the most effective observers of classroom practice as they have the most experience and training in classroom observation. However, there is much to be said for peer observation as it too provides strong evidence but also increases staff buy-in for the decisions that grow from the evaluation. Because the program evaluation team members may also be peers, it is essential to stress the importance of confidentiality, ensuring that what is seen in observations is not discussed outside of the evaluation team and that observers refrain from providing feedback to the teachers of the classrooms in which the observations are taking place. This is important because a program evaluation is about the program, not about an individual's performance.

When a number of observers are involved, the issue of inter-rater reliability needs to be considered. Inter-rater reliability exists when all of the observers make the same, or very close to the same, determinations no matter which of them does the observation (see page 71 for more information on inter-rater reliability). If there will be more than one observer, it is important that they have an opportunity to practice collecting the information and that they reach an agreement about how to record the observations. It may be helpful for the principal to set time aside to provide practice for team members using a volunteer teacher's classroom or videos of classroom instruction to practice data collection and calibration among all observers.

The evaluation team should consider the costs and benefits of including observations in the data collection plan. Observations can provide a helpful context to an evaluation, but they are time consuming. In many cases, an observation can provide valuable insight into how teachers are implementing a program, practice, or strategy, and how the learners are meeting program goals.

# Samples of Student Work

Student work provides rich data for many research questions having to do with classroom instruction. In a typical sampling process, one week of student work is collected from every classroom teacher whose practice would potentially be impacted by the results of the program evaluation. For example, if the question deals with math instruction in grades K–3, all math assignments from all teachers at those grade levels are collected. Evaluation team members look at each of these assignments and the student work produced to answer research questions such as whether the assignments are at grade level, or whether the grading is comparable from classroom to classroom.

# Documentary Evidence

Valuable data can also be gathered through an analysis of the written curriculum and pacing charts. This can reveal the degree to which curriculum aligns to state or Common Core standards, and the degree to which that curriculum is reflected in classroom instruction. In this analysis, the written curriculum is compared to the state or Common Core standards in a match-gap format to find out where any holes or redundancies exist. In a side-by-side comparison of the school or district curriculum to state or Common Core standards:

1. **Match.** By grade level, highlight on both your curriculum and state or Common Core standards documents those areas in which the knowledge and skills called for in your curriculum match those of Common Core standards.

2. **Gap.** By grade level, using a different color, highlight the state or Common Core standards document to show knowledge and skills called for in state or Common Core standards but not in your curriculum.

3. **Gap.** By grade level, using a third color, highlight your curriculum document to show knowledge and skills called for in your curriculum but not in state or Common Core standards.

Other documents can also provide valuable information. These include student learning data such as the results of statewide and local assessments (including teacher-made tests) and grades. *Documentary data* also includes contextual information such as retention, discipline, and attendance data.

Every data collection method has both advantages and challenges, as shown in table 2.1. The team will need to balance the need to obtain the best data to answer the questions with the constraints imposed by the limited available resources (including time and personnel) that can be set aside for the evaluation. Examples of survey, interview, and focus-group questions are included at the end of this chapter.

Table 2.1: Overview of Data Collection Methods

| Data Collection Method | Purpose | Advantages | Disadvantages |
|---|---|---|---|
| Surveys | To gather a lot of data in a short amount of time | Anonymous<br><br>Easy to show results in charts and graphs<br><br>Easy to compare and analyze results<br><br>Can be administered to large groups | Respondents may misunderstand questions.<br><br>Respondents may misunderstand scale.<br><br>Can seem impersonal<br><br>Can be expensive to translate into all languages of the school community |
| Interviews | To gather detailed perceptual information | Provides a deeper understanding of the issue from multiple perspectives<br><br>Builds trust between the interviewer and the respondent<br><br>Provides information on *how* and *why*<br><br>Provides an opportunity for the respondent to offer suggestions | Time consuming for the interviewer and the respondent<br><br>Difficult to analyze results<br><br>Difficult to quantify<br><br>Must train interviewers in the process |

| Data Collection Method | Purpose | Advantages | Disadvantages |
|---|---|---|---|
| Focus Groups | To gather data from groups with shared characteristics such as parents, students, or teachers | Can gather information about reactions to an experience or suggestion<br><br>May expose complaints or unanticipated information<br><br>Allows group members to build ideas from other members' comments<br><br>Particularly useful in situations in which trust is an issue or with groups who feel they have limited power | Need a facilitator and a recorder<br><br>Can be complex process to organize comments<br><br>Can be difficult to keep group on topic<br><br>May require an interpreter if focus-group respondents and facilitator do not share the same primary language |
| Classroom Observations | To gather data on classroom-based programs, practices, or strategies | Allows the team to view a program as it is actually occurring<br><br>Provides information on fidelity of implementation<br><br>Can increase staff buy-in to the evaluation<br><br>Allows the team to observe student response and behavior | Requires a well-designed and -understood observation process<br><br>Must provide observers with training, practice, and a well-designed rubric to ensure inter-rater reliability<br><br>Can be seen as intrusive by staff, especially if trust is an issue<br><br>Difficult to quantify |
| Samples of Student Work | To gather information about the cognitive demand and alignment to state or Common Core standards | Allows the team to study authentic student products<br><br>Grade-level or schoolwide samples ideal<br><br>Can provide a lens into teacher expectations<br><br>Can be launching point for lesson study | Requires commitment from teachers to submit all work products (not just those that are exemplary)<br><br>Can be difficult to generalize results if the sample size is too small<br><br>Requires that evaluators be knowledgeable about cognitive demand (see pages 51–52) and academic standards<br><br>Time consuming |
| Documenary Evidence | To provide information without interrupting the work and routine of the school | Can provide information on the way a program was intended to be implemented<br><br>Provides historical context<br><br>Can provide objective data, such as statewide assessment data<br><br>Can provide more detailed information than can be collected through other means | Data can be contradictory, out of date, or misleading.<br><br>The team may not know what documents are available.<br><br>May be difficult to analyze<br><br>May be difficult to quantify |

continued →

| Data Collection Method | Purpose | Advantages | Disadvantages |
|---|---|---|---|
| Curriculum Alignment | To determine the degree to which the school's curriculum, including unit and lesson plans and pacing guides, aligns with state or Common Core standards | Key to improving student achievement<br><br>Documents the alignment of written curriculum materials with standards<br><br>Identifies gaps in which supports are needed to facilitate a standards-based curriculum | Complex process<br><br>Time consuming<br><br>Requires that evaluators are knowledgeable about standards<br><br>Requires that all materials used by teachers are submitted for review |
| Alignment of Instructional Materials | To determine the degree to which textbooks and other instructional materials align with school, district, state, or Common Core standards | Key to improving instruction<br><br>Documents the alignment of instructional materials with standards<br><br>Identifies gaps in which materials are needed to support standards<br><br>Identifies extraneous or redundant materials | Requires that evaluators are knowledgeable about standards<br><br>Requires that all materials used by teachers are submitted for review<br><br>Time consuming<br><br>Can be expensive |

No single data source or collection method will (or should) provide all of the information needed to fully answer the research questions, nor will a single method provide enough data to make decisions on the basis of the evaluation's results. As your team considers how to collect the desired data, consider three key concepts: *generalizability, validity,* and *reliability* (each is described more fully on pages 71–73).

1. **Generalizability.** This is the degree to which conclusions based on the responses of a representative sample population can be extended to the population as a whole.

2. **Validity.** This addresses whether or not the data collection questions and instruments will actually measure what they are supposed to measure.

3. **Reliability.** This is the extent to which data gathering would yield the same results if the data were gathered from the same group of people a second or third time.

## Quantitative and Qualitative Data

When considering evidence for an evaluation, most people think of information that can be counted or measured numerically: student grades, standardized test scores, attendance records, student work, and so on. This is known as *quantitative* information or data. Quantitative data (see page 71) can be very useful because it is often easier to obtain and can be analyzed using familiar measures such as *mean, median,* and *mode* (see pages 68–69).

Descriptive data, such as beliefs about how or why a program or practice functions in a certain way, are known as *qualitative* (see page 72). These data, which are more difficult to measure, provide context and are valuable in designing program improvements. Examples of qualitative data collections include responses to the open-ended questions asked in focus groups and interviews.

A mix of measures, both quantitative and qualitative, forms a richer and more accurate picture. For example, using only one measure, such as overall school statewide assessment scores in math, might give the impression that the existing math program is resulting in high levels of student learning. However, additional measures might reveal other troubling data about the program. Surveys or interviews with students might also show that while students do well in math, they dislike the subject and have no idea how what they are learning in math relates to real life. Or it might reveal that while many students meet state standards, only 2 percent of students exceed state standards, and none of these are boys.

Collecting data is a little like walking on a tightrope: balance is key. The goal is to balance the need for information with the ease and cost of data collection. To do so, you must decide what information is critical to answering the questions. The evaluation team should prioritize the information to be gathered so that the evaluation can focus on the most vital data. The team needs to ensure that it gathers neither too much nor too little data. While a single data source will not provide enough data, too many sources can be overwhelming. What is collected should tightly address the research questions. You want just the right balance between the questions asked and the data collected to answer those questions.

## Data on Hand

In many cases, data needed for the program evaluation are already collected and readily available for use by the evaluation team. Such sources include the following:

- **Statewide student assessment data.** State assessment data are available in all states in reading and math and often in other subjects, such as writing and science. Data from these assessments are often disaggregated in a number of ways (for example, by racial, ethnic, special education, English learner, grade level, and gender groupings). These data need to be analyzed based on the program evaluation research questions. These data are available from your school, your district, or the state department of education.

- **School and district assessment data.** Many schools and districts have their own assessment systems aligned with state standards, such as MAPS®, Benchmark Tracker®, or other curriculum-based measures that employ direct observation and recording of a student's or class's performance as a basis for instructional decision making. Curriculum-based measures—for example, oral reading fluency measures—may be teacher, school, or district created, or commercially available, such as Dynamic Indicators of Basic Early Literacy Skills (DIBELS®). Their availability will differ from district to district. Start by asking the math, reading, or special education teachers at the school or the curriculum and assessment director at the school or district.

- **Attendance, dropout rates, and school safety data.** These are collected by the U.S. Department of Education for its annual reports and are available from the school, the district, and the state department of education.

- **Original goals and objectives of programs, practices, and strategies.** The original program goals can often be found in minutes of the school board or school council, in records relating to the original purchase of the product, or in the memories of staff members who participated in the original decision.

- **School climate survey data.** These data may be available from the school, state, or district.

- **School- and grade-level decision-making documents.** Information on decision making can sometimes be found in minutes from staff or grade-level meetings.

- **Classroom-based documents such as lesson plans, assessments, and student portfolios.** These data sources may be available schoolwide, or they may be found by contacting individual teachers.

- **Information about professional development provided for teachers.** These records are usually available at the school office or from the school or district curriculum director.

- **Expenditure data.** Data on finances are available at the school and district.

- **Grant reports.** These are usually kept on file in the school office for several years following the end of a grant.

Identifying the data collection methods gives us the information to fill in the fourth column of the blueprint, as shown in figure 2.9.

# Establishing Timelines Through Backward Construction

Next we turn to establishing project timelines. The first step is to decide when you need the evaluation results. Once you have identified the project due date, the evaluation team should begin to work on a timeline that builds backward from that date. Developing this schedule is often like fitting together pieces of a puzzle. For example, before you send a notice to parents requesting that they complete a survey, be sure to allocate time to develop the survey, test it out with a small pilot group, and prepare copies for distribution or for access via a web-based data collection tool.

Be realistic when assigning the amount of time needed—both in terms of labor hours and calendar time—for specific aspects of the evaluation. Planning too tightly almost guarantees that some tasks will fall behind, and the project overall may suffer. Build flexibility into the overall evaluation plan to allow for slippage. Set early deadlines in the timeline, and include some extra time near the due date.

## Make Calendars and Timelines Visible

After developing a master calendar of deadlines and timelines, determine how you will keep these important dates front and center in the minds of everyone working on the project. Consider posting a large calendar in a central area that includes important timelines and activities scheduled as part of the evaluation. In addition, you may want to use an electronic calendar program that can be quickly updated and shared with the team and the school as a whole. Automatic "tickler" or calendar alert functions can provide reminders as key dates approach.

When complete, add the timeline to the blueprint, as shown in figure 2.10 (page 28).

| Define Purpose | Select Program Evaluation Team | Determine Program Evaluation Research Questions | Identify Data Collection Methods | Establish Timelines | Assign Responsibilities | Identify Resources |
|---|---|---|---|---|---|---|
| The purpose of this program evaluation is to determine the degree to which our K–3 math program is resulting in students entering grade 4 math at grade level. | Principal: Jayne Tenn<br><br>Curriculum director: Jon Flint<br><br>Math coach: Judy Anderson<br><br>Grade-level chairs K–4:<br>Steve Mille<br>Nick Harnisch<br>Sabrina Black<br>Ashlee Grace<br>Pam Oki | A. What measures do our teachers use to determine what students know and are able to do in math at the end of grades K, 1, 2, and 3?<br><br>B. What measures do we use to determine what students know and are able to do in math at the beginning of grade 4?<br><br>C. Do all of these measures align with state or Common Core standards in math? | A. Collect results of assessment measures used in math in grades K, 1, 2, and 3.<br><br>B. Collect results of assessment measures in grade 4.<br><br>C1. Interview teachers to determine if the assessments are aligned to standards.<br><br>C2. Check with district to see if textbook alignment documents are available. | | | |

Figure 2.9: Sample evaluation blueprint, continued.

| Define Purpose | Select Program Evaluation Team | Determine Program Evaluation Research Questions | Identify Data Collection Methods | Establish Timelines | Assign Responsibilities | Identify Resources |
|---|---|---|---|---|---|---|
| The purpose of this program evaluation is to determine the degree to which our K–3 math program is resulting in students entering grade 4 math at grade level. | Principal: Jayne Tenn<br><br>Curriculum director: Jon Flint<br><br>Math coach: Judy Anderson<br><br>Grade-level chairs K–4:<br>Steve Mille<br>Nick Harnisch<br>Sabrina Black<br>Ashlee Grace<br>Pam Oki | A. What measures do our teachers use to determine what students know and are able to do in math at the end of grades K, 1, 2, and 3?<br><br>B. What measures do we use to determine what students know and are able to do in math at the beginning of grade 4?<br><br>C. Do all of these measures align with state or Common Core standards in math? | A. Collect results of assessment measures used in math in grades K, 1, 2, and 3.<br><br>B. Collect results of assessment measures in grade 4.<br><br>C1. Interview teachers to determine if the assessments are aligned to standards.<br><br>C2. Check with district to see if textbook alignment documents are available. | A. Second week in October<br><br>B. Second week in October<br><br>C1. Third and fourth weeks in October<br><br>C2. Second week in October | | |

Figure 2.10: Sample evaluation blueprint, continued.

# Assigning Responsibilities

The next step in the blueprint is to assign responsibilities for the action steps defined thus far. Some program evaluation responsibilities, such as "interview teachers to determine if the assessments are aligned to standards" (C1 in figures 2.9 and 2.10) or those assigned to more than one team member, may require more detailed planning than can be easily accommodated on the blueprint. It may be useful to include a more detailed level of planning or sketch that describes how each step will be carried out and by whom.

If this is the case in your program evaluation, the sketch shown in figure 2.11 will provide an additional level of detail by laying out who is responsible for what in complex or multifaceted program evaluations. If this tool seems useful to you in your program evaluation, begin by listing the research questions and data collection methods from the blueprint at the top of the sketch template. Then list the tasks that need to be carried out, when, and by whom. Since slightly different information will be collected in every evaluation, add and subtract rows and columns to match the evaluation at hand. Once complete, this becomes an addendum to the blueprint. Be sure to add the first start date and the last end date from the sketches to the blueprint so that these more complicated tasks are transparent within the blueprint.

| Program evaluation research question(s): | | | |
|---|---|---|---|
| Data collection methods: | | | |
| **Task** | **Begin/End** | **Lead** | **Team Members** |
| Conduct parent focus groups, and organize results. | | | |
| Conduct teacher interviews, and organize results. | | | |
| Review curriculum materials, and organize results. | | | |
| Review student work, and organize results. | | | |
| Observe classrooms, and organize results. | | | |

Figure 2.11: Task sketch template.

For work that remains unassigned after the initial matching of tasks to the evaluation team, look first to other school and district staff members to take on these tasks. The advantage of using existing staff members is that they are on-site during specific times and days, so planning work is easier. Consider providing substitutes to free up staff members as necessary. Stipends or extra-duty pay will be necessary to compensate staff members who put in extra hours before and after school. If staff resources are not available, consider asking for help from sources such as the district office, staff members who have recently retired, parents or community members, or outside consultants.

These duty assignments are then entered into column six of the blueprint, as shown in figure 2.12 (page 30).

| Define Purpose | Select Program Evaluation Team | Determine Program Evaluation Research Questions | Identify Data Collection Methods | Establish Timelines | Assign Responsibilities | Identify Resources |
|---|---|---|---|---|---|---|
| The purpose of this program evaluation is to determine the degree to which our K–3 math program is resulting in students entering grade 4 math at grade level. | Principal: Jayne Tenn<br><br>Curriculum director: Jon Flint<br><br>Math coach: Judy Anderson<br><br>Grade-level chairs K–4:<br>Steve Mille<br>Nick Harnisch<br>Sabrina Black<br>Ashlee Grace<br>Pam Oki | A. What measures do our teachers use to determine what students know and are able to do in math at the end of grades K, 1, 2, and 3?<br><br>B. What measures do we use to determine what students know and are able to do in math at the beginning of grade 4?<br><br>C. Do all of these measures align with state or Common Core standards in math? | A. Collect results of assessment measures used in math in grades K, 1, 2, and 3.<br><br>B. Collect results of assessment measures in grade 4.<br><br>C1. Interview teachers to determine if the assessments are aligned to standards.<br><br>C2. Check with district to see if textbook alignment documents are available. | A. Second week in October<br><br>B. Second week in October<br><br>C1. Third and fourth weeks in October<br><br>C2. Second week in October | A. Judy<br><br>B. Judy<br><br>C1. Steve, Nick, Sabrina, Ashlee<br><br>C2. Jon | |

Figure 2.12: Sample evaluation blueprint, continued.

# Identifying Resources

Although you may already have had some discussions about the resources available for the project, at this stage it is important to begin to identify the resources to be allocated for the evaluation. In this step, the principal and evaluation team look at the tasks outlined in the blueprint and create a close estimate of the costs that will be entailed in carrying out each. For example, when estimating costs for surveys, include postage, copying, and the time that will be required for data entry. If release time or extra-duty pay will be needed to analyze the survey data, be sure to build in those expenses. Because you have already assigned responsibilities for each task, employee costs can be easily estimated.

Sometimes, assigning the costs to the tasks reveals that the evaluation is more expensive than expected. This is a good time to make a final check on the financial feasibility of the project and to make any adjustments. For example, the evaluation team may have planned to send surveys to the parents of all students in the school. But when the team estimates the costs of printing, mailing, and entering the results into spreadsheets by hand, it may rethink that aspect of the project. Perhaps electronic surveys or a series of focus groups could provide similar information at a lower cost.

This step is a project milestone. The team is now ready to complete the blueprint. An example of what a section of the completed blueprint might look like is shown in figure 2.13 (page 32).

# What if Something Gets Off Track?

Part of the planning process is to think through possible bumps in the road so that you can avoid them. However, not all problems, disruptions, or barriers can be anticipated, so it is helpful to consider what to do if something does go wrong. Keep the following concepts in mind when you plan for problems—or when one arises unexpectedly.

## Make Trade-Offs

Develop a clear understanding of what the evaluation must accomplish. On occasion, some data may prove to be unavailable. If the loss of these data will not significantly detract from the evaluation, report to the team and move forward. Sometimes you may have to accept a trade-off between completing the evaluation on time and extending the timelines in order to incorporate all the data you want.

## Be Flexible

Adapt as necessary to support the goals of the evaluation. For example, if it becomes apparent after the first few interviews that the questions are not getting at the data needed, consider rewriting the questions to better glean the needed information.

Planning and adhering to the plan saves time and avoids confusion. Plans and timelines do occasionally need to be adjusted when responding to unforeseen difficulties. Before making that decision, however, first consider how the project could still be completed within the timelines set. Activities tend to be interrelated, and amending timelines for one part of the project may have an adverse effect on another part of the project.

| Define Purpose | Select Program Evaluation Team | Determine Program Evaluation Research Questions | Identify Data Collection Methods | Establish Timelines | Assign Responsibilities | Identify Resources |
|---|---|---|---|---|---|---|
| The purpose of this program evaluation is to determine the degree to which our K–3 math program is resulting in students entering grade 4 math at grade level. | Principal: Jayne Tenn<br><br>Curriculum director: Jon Flint<br><br>Math coach: Judy Anderson<br><br>Grade-level chairs<br><br>K–4:<br>Steve Mille<br>Nick Harnisch<br>Sabrina Black<br>Ashlee Grace<br>Pam Oki | A. What measures do our teachers use to determine what students know and are able to do in math at the end of grades K, 1, 2, and 3?<br><br>B. What measures do we use to determine what students know and are able to do in math at the beginning of grade 4?<br><br>C. Do all of these measures align with state or Common Core standards in math? | A. Collect results of assessment measures used in math in grades K, 1, 2, and 3.<br><br>B. Collect results of assessment measures in grade 4.<br><br>C1. Interview teachers to determine if the assessments are aligned to standards.<br><br>C2. Check with district to see if textbook alignment documents are available. | A. Second week in October<br><br>B. Second week in October<br><br>C1. Third and fourth weeks in October<br><br>C2. Second week in October | A. Judy<br><br>B. Judy<br><br>C1. Steve, Nick, Sabrina, Ashlee<br><br>C2. Jon | A. None (can be accomplished as part of current assignment)<br><br>B. None (can be accomplished as part of current assignment)<br><br>C1. Eight days substitute pay (2 days @ $165.00 per day x 4 teachers = $1,320.00)<br><br>C2. None (can be accomplished as part of current assignment) |

Figure 2.13: Sample evaluation blueprint, completed.

# Moving From Planning to Doing

With the blueprint complete, it's time to move from planning for the evaluation to executing the action steps. For those evaluations that call for the collection of data such as surveys, interviews, focus groups, or observations, the next chapter will provide the information needed to create and administer those tools to net just the right information needed to answer the program evaluation questions.

# Gathering Data

Once the planning is complete and the blueprint drafted, the data collection phase of the program evaluation can begin. While not every program evaluation will make use of surveys, interviews, focus groups, or observational data, many will. This chapter will focus on how to create and use these specific data collection tools, but you may consider many other forms of data, such as curriculum data and student work and assessment data.

Start by looking at your blueprint to see what information will be collected and what tools will be used to collect it. It also helps to think ahead to the data analysis phase (discussed in chapter 4) since that might provide some clues that help refine the data collection tasks.

## Multiple Data Points

In order to avoid making decisions using limited data or a single data point, sufficient data must be collected from multiple sources to answer each question. For example:

- Grade-level student-assessment data from multiple classrooms

- Parent surveys

- Classroom observation data from multiple classrooms and via multiple observers

- Student work analyses from multiple classrooms and grade levels

Only after evidence is collected from at least two different sources and not contradicted by any other data is the evidence deemed sufficient for decision making.

## Developing Surveys

Knowing what information you need to collect is half the battle. When creating surveys, the other half is constructing questions that will provide the information you need. In interviews and focus groups, if a question or a response is unclear, it can be explained further. That option is not available in surveys, and surveys therefore require additional upfront planning and thinking about how questions should be phrased. For example, if the survey is designed to collect data about individual grade levels, parents will need to complete a different survey for each grade level in which they have students. Surveys will therefore need to be boldly marked so it is clear that the results pertain to a specific grade level. Following is a list of other tips for developing an effective survey:

- Make the questions short and clear, ideally no more than twenty words. Be sure to give the respondents all the information they will need to answer the questions.

- Avoid questions that have more than one central idea or theme.

- Keep questions relevant to the problem.

- Do not use jargon. Your target population must be able to answer the questions you are asking. If they are not familiar with the profession's vocabulary or acronyms, do not use them.

- Avoid words that are not exact (for example, *generally, usually, average, typically, often,* and *rarely*). If you do use these words, you may get information that is unreliable or not useful.

- Avoid stating questions in the negative.

- Avoid introducing bias. Slanted questions will produce slanted results.

- Make sure the answer to one question relates smoothly to the next. For example, if necessary add "if yes . . . did you?" or "if no . . . did you?"

- Give exact instructions to the respondent on how to record answers. For example, explain exactly where to write the answers: check a box, circle a number, and so forth.

- Provide response alternatives. For example, include the response *other* for answers that don't fit elsewhere.

- Make the questionnaire attractive. Plan its format carefully, using subheadings, spaces, and boxes.

- Make the survey look easy for a respondent to complete. An unusually long questionnaire may alarm respondents.

- Decide beforehand how the answers will be recorded and analyzed. (W. K. Kellogg Foundation, 2004, pp. 80–81)

Figure 3.1 presents a variety of sample items that might be included in teacher, staff, parent, and student surveys.

Note also the happy face and sad face in the survey example. These are important visual cues to help respondents see that the scale runs from positive to negative. Scales commonly run from either best to worst or vice versa. Respondents who do not read the directions carefully may mark the answers in just the opposite way they intended. Unsurprisingly, this has serious consequences in data analysis.

| | Strongly Agree ☺ | Agree | Not Sure | Disagree | Strongly Disagree ☹ | Not Applicable |
|---|---|---|---|---|---|---|
| **Sample Teacher Survey Items** | | | | | | |
| Teachers use formative assessments in math to identify student skill levels. | | | | | | |
| Students find my math classes rigorous and challenging. | | | | | | |
| Instructional time is protected from interruption by noninstructional activities, such as announcements and assemblies. | | | | | | |
| **Sample Educational Assistant Survey Items** | | | | | | |
| Students understand what their teachers expect them to know and be able to do in each lesson. | | | | | | |
| I am included and participate in grade-level math planning meetings. | | | | | | |
| **Sample Parent Survey Items** | | | | | | |
| My child's math class challenges him or her academically. | | | | | | |
| School staff members have high expectations for responsible student behavior. | | | | | | |
| **Sample Student Survey Items (Grades 5 and 6)** | | | | | | |
| I feel there is at least one adult in this school who cares about me. | | | | | | |
| My teachers help me understand why what I'm learning in school is important. | | | | | | |

Figure 3.1: Sample survey items.

## Tips for Parent Surveys

The deadline for return of the survey should be included on each survey and formatted to be visually prominent. Two weeks is about right for most survey response turnarounds. Late survey returns are problematic because they may come in after the data have been quantified. It is best to decide in advance what is going to be done about survey results that arrive after the due date. If late returns will not be considered, it is wise to include a statement to that effect in the survey instructions.

Since you need to receive as many completed surveys as possible, be sure to include a note at the beginning of the survey that explains the survey's importance for program improvement efforts. Include a contact or email address to which questions about the survey can be addressed. As discussed previously, respondents must feel safe in responding honestly to survey questions. In the instructions for the survey, include an explanation of how respondents' anonymity will be guaranteed.

Finally, include instructions on how to return the survey, or, if it is a hard-copy survey, a self-addressed stamped envelope. Mailed surveys from the school usually get good returns, but as postage rates increase, it can be an expensive proposition. Even so, it is best not to send the surveys home with students as they often do not make it into the hands of parents.

Electronic surveys can be very effective. There are many free or inexpensive web- and software-based survey-creation tools available, for example: Moodle (http://moodle.org), Survey Monkey® (www.surveymonkey.com), Survey Gizmo™ (www.surveygizmo.com), or Zoomerang® (www.zoomerang.com). There are many of these tools available, but take care to ensure the tool you select (especially if you select a free tool) either has charting and graphing capability built in or the survey results can be easily exported to a spreadsheet program, like Microsoft Excel, in which graphs and charts are easy to create. You may already have a program at your school that has this capability, or your district may have access to these tools and perhaps even have someone on staff who can help create the survey.

Even if the surveys are available electronically, it is necessary to have some hard-copy versions if the survey is to be sent home to those parents who do not have access to the Internet. Your school (or parent teacher association) very likely has a list of parents who prefer to be contacted by email and those who do not.

If the response rate is low after the first few days, consider a follow-up email or text message reminding survey recipients of its importance.

## Tips for Staff Surveys

Paper versions of staff surveys can often be completed during staff meetings, and asking members to turn in their surveys as they leave will ensure a strong response. Some teachers will request additional time to think about and complete the surveys. Two to three days should be adequate in this case. If surveys are to be placed in staff mailboxes or distributed to all staff members along with morning announcements, it is best to allow a little more response time. One week is normally adequate. Be sure the form clearly indicates where to turn in completed surveys and reminds users not to include names or personally identifiable information.

Many schools have used web-based surveys, especially with staff. Just as with parent surveys, web-based staff surveys offer distinct advantages. Electronic surveys save more than just paper. They save time for school staff members who would otherwise have to duplicate, distribute, and collect paper surveys. Electronic surveys also save time in tabulating and displaying results. However, electronic surveys are not a panacea. A poorly designed online survey offers no advantages over a poorly designed paper survey. One disadvantage to online surveys is that respondents may believe that their responses will not be anonymous because a log-in is often required to access the surveys. Respondents may fear that through the log-in, surveys may be traced to individual respondents. This is a particularly important consideration when looking at a program, practice, or strategy that is controversial, or when trust is an issue for staff or community members. If this is the case, a paper-based survey will be more likely to result in frank and honest responses.

## Processing Completed Surveys

For each of the methods of data collection, someone will need to keep track of what has been finished and what is still awaiting completion. Have all the surveys been returned? Have all the interviews been completed? An electronic spreadsheet can be used for this type of monitoring.

# Creating Interview and Focus-Group Questions

Interviews and focus groups offer the opportunity to delve into the research questions at a deeper level. Following are some tips that will aid in the creation and administration of interview and focus-group questions:

- **Ask open-ended questions.** Ask questions that encourage respondents to explain and elaborate—avoid using yes/no questions. Questions that begin with *how* are particularly effective. For example, ask, "How has the school or district provided teachers with professional development in math?" not, "Has the school or district provided teachers with professional development in math?"

- **Avoid absolutes.** Because respondents may avoid choosing extremes, do not use words such as *all, always, none, never, just, only,* or *unfairly.*

- **Avoid bias.** Ask questions that do not lead respondents to answer in a particular way. Ask, "How effective do you believe the recently implemented math program is with your students?" not, "There are many teachers who believe the recently implemented math program is effective. Do you agree?"

- **Include only one topic per question.** Questions that address more than one topic may confuse participants, leading them to answer only one part of the question or to answer neither part, and there is no way for the evaluation team to tell when this has occurred. The solution is to separate two ideas into two questions. For example, first ask, "What would make instruction in our recently adopted geometry program more effective?" followed by, "What would make instruction in our recently adopted algebra program more effective?" rather than asking only, "What would make instruction in geometry and algebra more effective?"

- **Avoid questions that are confusing or too long.** Refrain from asking questions that are so general that the respondent has to figure out what the questions might mean. Additionally, avoid questions so long that the respondent forgets what was asked at the beginning of the question by the time the interviewer reads the end of the question.

- **Ask for elaboration.** Even well-written focus-group or interview questions can sometimes result in an answer that is too short to provide much information. In these cases, ask follow-up questions such as "Can you give an example of a time when . . . ?" or "Can you tell me a little more about . . . ?"

- **Ask fewer, better questions.** It is better to ask fewer questions that are essential to the data collection than to ask more questions that, while interesting, are not vital to the program evaluation. There must be plenty of time in the interview or focus group to explore the questions posed so that neither the interviewer nor the respondent feels rushed to finish in the time allotted.

Figure 3.2 presents sample questions that might be used in teacher, student, or family interviews or focus groups. Each question should be tightly aligned to the evaluation research question and clearly written to ensure that the team will get the information it needs to answer the research question. For example, if the team is trying to determine the amount of time students are receiving math instruction each week, which of the following questions would be most likely to produce the data the team needs?

1. How many times each week do you teach math?

2. Is math taught to every student each day by every teacher?

3. How many minutes per week do you teach mathematics?

Question three is the best choice. Question one uncovers how often math is taught by the teacher, but it assumes that every teacher devotes the same amount of time to the lesson. Question two, assumes that teachers know exactly what is happening in other teachers' classrooms, and may additionally lead the interview into topics that are outside those of the evaluation. Question three will provide the data that can be used to answer the question and will, as a bonus, provide quantitative data too.

It is a good idea to pilot the questions with a few people outside the evaluation team before the questions are finalized to ensure that respondents will understand the question as written and that the responses received will provide the information you need to collect.

| Sample Teacher Interview and Focus-Group Questions | |
|---|---|
| How do you determine the math level of your students? | |
| What math programs are in place for the lowest- and highest-performing students? | |
| What data do you have on the success of these programs with children in your class? | |
| How many minutes per week do you teach mathematics? | |
| **Sample Student Interview and Focus-Group Questions (Grades 4–6)** | |
| What do you like about math? | |
| What is hard about math? | |
| What kind of math homework do you do? | |
| **Sample Family Interview and Focus-Group Questions** | |
| What information does the school give you about your child's progress in learning math? | |
| Is the math program challenging for your child? | (Note the number of *yes* and number of *no* responses here.) |
| What are some examples of challenging math assignments? | |

Figure 3.2: Sample interview and focus-group questions.

# Using Classroom Observations

Observations allow the program evaluation team members to look at the behaviors, interactions, and environment associated with the program, practice, or strategy being reviewed. The following tips will be helpful when observation is an element of the evaluation:

- **Determine the focus.** Think about the research questions you plan to answer through observation and about the focus of your data collection. For example, you may want to know the degree to which a specific questioning strategy is being implemented during math instruction. The focus of the observation might be on looking and listening for evidence of the use of the strategy, the cognitive demands of the classroom interactions, the skill of the teacher in using the strategy, or certain student behaviors.

- **Design a system for data collection.** The next step is to decide exactly how the observation data will be collected and recorded. Two of the most common are:

  a. *Checklists (quantitative).* These tools are used to gather quantifiable data during an observation. To create an observation checklist, design a template with the research question at the top of the page and a list of look-fors that if present would demonstrate the degree to which a specific strategy, practice, or behavior is evident during the observation. Figure 3.3 shows an example of such a classroom observation tool.

    b. *Running records (qualitative).* In this data collection methodology, observers take sequential notes describing what they see and hear during the observation. They gather evidence about what the students are hearing, saying, doing, and learning. Whenever possible, without interrupting instruction, observers interact with students, asking open-ended questions aligned with the research questions.

- **Determine the number of observations.** Based on the research questions, determine how many and which classes or other areas should be observed as part of the data collection. While not all classes need to be observed, the observations must result in a sample large enough to ensure that the data collection accurately portrays the program, practice, or strategy that is the subject of the evaluation.

- **Timing is everything.** It is critical that you schedule your observations so that you are observing the activity that is the focus of your research question. Arriving to observe math questioning strategies during reading instruction will not answer the evaluation questions. This requires that a schedule be determined in advance of the observations.

| Look-Fors | Yes | No | Undetermined | Notes |
|---|---|---|---|---|
| The teacher uses questioning strategies that elicit a range of intellectual behavior (remember, understand, apply, analyze, evaluate, create). | | | | |
| Classroom assignments are rigorous and contribute to student understanding. | | | | |
| Remedial, intervention, and lower-level classes or groupings are engaging and challenging. | | | | |

Figure 3.3: Sample classroom evaluation tool.

# Training Data Collectors

Evaluation team members who will act as observers and interviewers will need to be trained to ensure that the process and data collection are consistent regardless of which team member is collecting the data. In the training session, the following information should be covered (Paulsen & Dailey, 2002):

- **Context.** Discuss the purpose of the evaluation as well as program goals, objectives, and expectations.

- **Shared understandings.** Discuss the instruments to be used and their purposes. Ensure there is shared understanding of the exact meaning of each question or look-for on the data collection instrument.

- **Standardization.** All data collection should be the same, no matter who is gathering the data. For example, decide in advance if follow-up questions in interviews are allowed, if extra time will be allotted should an interview take longer than expected, or how the office staff should respond if parents contact them about the meaning of survey questions.

- **Demonstration and practice.** Before undertaking the data collection, the team members involved should pilot any written materials, such as surveys with other team members who have not been part of the survey creation. Interview and focus-group questions and processes should also be practiced to be sure that all data are captured accurately and that the interviewer or observer closely follows the protocols.

- **Behavior.** Discuss issues such as confidentiality, timeliness, and approaching the work as a learner.

# Ensuring Confidentiality

Candid responses are an important component of accurate data collection. Therefore, respondents should be assured that their answers will be kept confidential. In some cases, you may need to take special steps to provide for anonymous data collection. Because at the school level there may be only "a small number of participants and key stakeholders [who] may be easily identified, evaluators must ensure that all information is anonymous or that the identities of those who provided information are kept secret from external parties. By doing so, participants are protected and the integrity of the data is maintained" (Carr, 2004, p. 5).

The evaluation team and data collectors should be discreet and professional with all information they obtain. No participants in the evaluation should suffer negative consequences for expressing their opinions, ideas, or thoughts.

Once all of the tasks have been assigned, the instruments designed, and training accomplished, it is time to begin the data collection. It is good to have regular team meetings during the data collection time frame to ensure it is going as planned and that no unforeseen problems have arisen. At least one team member should be keeping his or her eye on the timeline to ensure that the data collection is going as planned. Next, the team will turn its attention to the analysis of the data.

# 4

# Analyzing the Data

Once the evidence has been collected, the most exciting time of a program evaluation has arrived: it is now possible to begin drawing conclusions from the evidence. The evaluation team will now take stock of and organize the collected data, look for trends, ensure the data are corroborated, and begin to think about how to display the data so that answers to the evaluation questions emerge.

## What Data Do We Have?

The team begins the data analysis by examining the data collected to ensure that all the evidence pertinent to the evaluation questions has been gathered. Here the evaluation team answers questions such as:

- What information do we have?

- How should we organize it?

- Does the information answer our questions?

- Are we missing any data that we said we would collect in the blueprint?

If changes were made to the evidence collection methodology, or if one or more data collection methods were dropped altogether, the team must consider the effect that loss of data will have on the team's ability to answer the research questions. If you discover that data crucial to fully understanding the picture as a whole have not been captured, it may be necessary to plan to collect that information.

The team also should keep in mind the context in which the data were collected. Perhaps data were not collected as planned because two teachers were absent on the day their classrooms were scheduled for observation, and substitute teachers taught those classes. Or perhaps the survey regarding school discipline was administered right after a fight in the cafeteria, and some members of the team believe timing may have skewed the results. By considering context, the evaluation team can make better-informed decisions about the *reliability* and *validity* (see pages 72–73) of the information.

This is a critical time for the principal to remind the team members how important it is to be objective when analyzing the data. Although their membership in the school community means that evaluation team members come to the evaluation process with unique understandings about the school's culture and processes, they also may come as supporters—or detractors—of the program, practice, or strategy being evaluated. Their roles as members of the evaluation team demand that their own opinions not affect the analysis of the data.

# Organizing the Data

The team will need to take the raw findings and incorporate them into a coherent statement about the efficacy of the program being studied. It may be helpful to display some data graphically—for example, the team may use a pie chart to show how much of the school day is devoted to math across all grade levels, or a bar chart to show the differences in the amount of time devoted to math at each grade level or classroom. In any case, the team needs to ensure that the information and supporting data are easy to understand.

Different types of data require different analytical approaches. Quantitative data can be organized into numerical ratings. For example, if the team uses a five-point survey scale from *Strongly Disagree* through *Strongly Agree*, the results are commonly organized by the number and percentage of responses (that is, the proportion of respondents that selected a particular answer) in each category as shown in figure 4.1.

| | Strongly Agree ☺ | Agree | Not Sure | Disagree | Strongly Disagree ☹ | Not Applicable |
|---|---|---|---|---|---|---|
| My child's math class is challenging. (Total responses: 60) | 12 (20%) | 32 (53%) | 2 (3%) | 8 (13%) | 4 (7%) | 2 (3%) |

Note: Because the figures are rounded to the nearest whole number, the percentages might not add to an even 100%.

Figure 4.1: Five-point survey data organized into numerical ratings.

Percentages are often reported by grouping categories so that trends are more easily seen. In figure 4.2, the *Agree* column combines all responses from the *Strongly Agree* and *Agree* columns. The *Disagree* column combines all responses from the *Strongly Disagree* and *Disagree* columns. The *Not Sure or Not Applicable* column combines all responses from the *Not Sure* and *Not Applicable* columns.

| | Agree | Disagree | Not Sure or Not Applicable |
|---|---|---|---|
| My child's math class is challenging. | 73% | 20% | 6% |

Figure 4.2: Condensed five-point survey data.

Qualitative data, such as responses to open-ended questions in interviews and focus groups, must also be organized into groupings so that they can be analyzed. These groupings may be as simple as *concerns about the program*, *support for the program*, *suggestions for improving the program*, and *comments that pertain to areas outside this evaluation*. Once the responses are organized, trends can be grouped and displayed.

## Conflicting Data

Sometimes data from one source conflict with data from another source. Conflicting data should be reported, along with the sources of the conflict. For example, "78 percent of teachers believed their math classes challenged students, while 42 percent of parents and 31 percent of students felt those math classes were challenging." Often these apparent conflicts reveal important information that the evaluation team needs to consider. This is a good reason not to base findings on one type or source of data. In the previous example, the data reported are all perceptual as reported on surveys. Again, a well-designed evaluation will always build in multiple data sources so that answers to research questions come from at least two (and three are even better) kinds of data collection. More information about the challenge present in math classes could be drawn from classroom observations, student interviews, the alignment of instruction to the written curriculum, and the level of cognitive demand present in student assignments.

# Analyzing the Data

In the data analysis stage, the team examines the evidence in a way that supports decision making about the program. The raw data may seem confusing or overwhelming to those outside the process. Therefore, one of the evaluation team's key responsibilities is to bring order to data.

A good way to approach this is to divide the evaluation team into small subgroups. For example, two or three team members may be assigned to closely examine the survey results for trends and conclusions that could be drawn from those data, while another subgroup looks at the results of focus groups and interviews, another at student work, another at assessment data, and so on. Ask each subgroup to look at its data and answer the following four questions:

1. Do these results make sense? What do they contribute to our understanding of the program, practice, or strategy being evaluated?

2. What do the data reveal?

3. What questions do the data evoke?

4. How can the data be displayed?

This phase can be a little messy. The key to success is not to rush the evaluation process. The first fact discovered may not be the most important one. Don't make too much of small differences between groups or overgeneralize the findings. The team's findings should reflect only the data gathered and analyzed in the evaluation (Cicchinelli & Barley, 1999; W. K. Kellogg Foundation, 2004).

# What Do the Data Mean?

Once the evaluation team subgroups have organized their data, each subgroup works to corroborate the data and to tease out from the data the most important findings, trends, and results. Next, each group consolidates this information and prepares it to be shared with the rest of the evaluation team. Then the entire evaluation team comes together to begin to integrate the pieces into a cohesive whole. First, the team reviews the evaluation purpose statement and program evaluation research questions. Then each subgroup presents its most important findings to the group as a whole. After all subgroups have been heard, the group focuses on four questions:

1. Do we see answers to our questions in the data?

2. Are themes emerging from the data that are so strong that we should highlight them in the analysis?

3. How can we organize the research data into coherent displays?

4. What questions remain to be answered?

This analysis is similar to working a jigsaw puzzle. The evaluation team will need to take individual data elements and begin to piece them together to create a larger picture of the program. Again, it is important for the evaluation team to maintain an objective view of the results and to systematically consider all explanations for the results. Before moving into making recommendations about the program being reviewed, the team should do the following:

• Review its documentation and be sure that the information and data are complete.

• Determine if it has answered every research question to the best of its ability.

• Be sure the information and data are organized in a way that leaves no lingering questions in the minds of the review team members.

# Displaying the Data

The data display is important to make the data analysis more understandable to various audiences. Be selective about which data are displayed. The most pressing consideration is that the displays provide the audience with guidance on what data are most important and why. Simply having data is not a good reason to include them in the report. If the choice comes down to choosing between spending time on the data displays or on the analysis, prioritize the analysis, and go for simple, straightforward displays that illustrate only the most important findings from the analysis.

Possible types of graphic displays include those in the following list. For more information about charts and graphs, see page 69.

- **Table.** In this display, the data are displayed numerically or in percentages in rows and columns that correspond to the questions asked and responses given.

|  | Agree | Disagree | Not Sure or Not Applicable |
|---|---|---|---|
| My child's math class is challenging. | 73% | 20% | 6% |
| School staff members have high expectations for responsible student behavior. | 65% | 31% | 4% |

- **Bar graph.** This type of graph consists of separate bars that represent different parts of the whole. The length or height of each bar represents the quantity within that part.

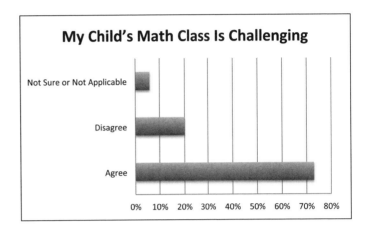

- **Pie chart.** This is a circular chart used to compare parts of the whole. It is divided into sections that are proportional in size to the quantity represented.

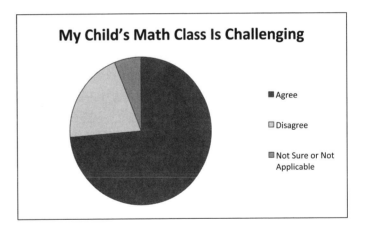

- **Line graph.** This type of graph displays the relationship between two types of information, such as the percentage of students meeting math standards.

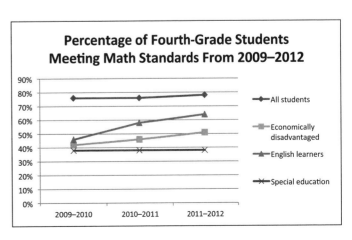

Displaying information in graphs or charts can help clarify the meaning of the data. Consider using graphical representations during the analysis phase of the project as well as in formal evaluation reports, but don't limit the data to quantitative results. When working with the qualitative data, direct quotes help succinctly characterize teacher, parent, or student opinion and both enliven and personalize the report. These can have a substantially greater impact than an analysis of quantitative data alone as they provide the *why* behind the support or nonsupport of the program, practice, or strategy.

## Statewide Student Assessment Data

Statewide assessment data are best displayed in charts, graphs, or tables. While there are many ways to look at and analyze statewide student achievement data, two common sets of data to display for program evaluation purposes are:

1. **Current data.** Limit these displays to the subject area and grade levels included in the evaluation. Examine how all students achieved on the assessment, and compare and contrast with how relevant groups (such as students who are English learners, special education, or impoverished) achieved.

2. **Trends over time.** It is ideal if the analysis can look at student achievement in the years in which the program, practice, or strategy has been in place at the school, as well as the time preceding.

## Survey Data

If surveys are administered during the evaluation process, they will need to be collected, tallied, and the results reported. For paper-based surveys, it is easy, though time consuming, to compile the data and create reports using a spreadsheet program. Tally the responses using a copy of the original survey form, and then transfer the questions along with the data into the spreadsheet. Since the data will be analyzed based on what is entered, all data entries must be double-checked for accuracy prior to the data analysis. Electronic survey programs will automatically complete this step. If the electronic survey program you are using has limited or no charting or graphing capability, you may want to move the results into a spreadsheet program with these features built in.

If you are using a table format, display the data for each question by showing the number and percentage of responses in each of the response categories (*Strongly Agree, Agree,* and so on). Always be sure to include the question with the results. Figure 4.1 (page 46) an example of this strategy.

## Student Work

If student work is collected for analysis, the team will review each assignment and the resulting student work and record two distinct pieces of data to display:

1. The level of cognitive demand in terms of Bloom's Revised Taxonomy of Educational Objectives (Anderson & Krathwohl, 2001) (see page 70)

2. An evaluation of the level of rigor present in relation to state or Common Core standards

Reporting of student work begins with an accounting of the total number of assignments received from which teachers at which grade levels. In the following example, an analysis of student work in math over a period of one week was collected from eighteen K–4 teachers. In this case, a total of eighty-five unique assignments were received and reviewed. A *unique assignment* is one that is given in one or more classes. Thus, identical assignments given in three classes at the same grade level count as a single unique assignment. These data are best displayed as charts, graphs, or tables (such as that displayed in figure 4.3) so that the results are easy to read and understand.

| Grade Level | Number of Unique Assignments (Total Assignments Received: 85) |
|---|---|
| K | 9 |
| 1 | 16 |
| 2 | 21 |
| 3 | 18 |
| 4 | 21 |

Figure 4.3: Breakdown of a collection of student work reviewed by grade level.

Another way to report on student work is to display data on the cognitive demand (sometimes referred to as *depth of knowledge*) required by each assignment. *Cognitive demand* refers to the kind or level of knowledge a student must demonstrate in order to complete the assignment. Each assignment is matched to descriptors that help distinguish between types of understanding. For example, some assignments may require students to demonstrate an understanding of what they have learned by recalling or reciting facts, such as remembering the definition of *volume*. Other assignments might display a higher level of cognitive demand, such as requiring students to use knowledge to solve problems (for example, calculating how many marbles could fit in a one-liter jar), to apply what has been learned to make decisions about new situations, or to predict the results of certain courses of action.

To determine the cognitive demand of an assignment, compare each assignment to a classification system, such as those in Anderson and Krathwohl's (2001) Bloom's Revised Taxonomy of Educational Objectives (page 70). There are a number of high-quality taxonomic systems that can be used for this purpose. If your school or district uses another classification system, use that one in the steps below. If your school or district has not adopted a classification system, consider using Bloom's Revised Taxonomy as it lends itself particularly well to evaluation of student work. This classification system divides tasks into two orders representing *higher-* and *lower-order* thinking skills with three progressively more complex levels in each of the orders. Within the lower order, the cognitive demand progresses in complexity from remembering to understanding to applying. Within the higher order, the cognitive demand progresses from analysis to evaluation to creating. When assignments call for a mix of cognitive demands, or if an assignment could fit in more than one level, it is placed at the highest demonstrated level of cognitive demand. For example, if an assignment required students to *remember* details of a historical event (a lower-order cognitive demand) and then *evaluate* competing interpretations (a higher-order cognitive demand), it would be considered a higher-order assignment. If the team is unable to determine the level of the assignment, it is listed as *could not be determined.*

In the following example, the analysis of student work showed that the majority (sixty-six of eighty-five assignments, or 78 percent) was targeted at lower-order thinking skills, and the greatest percentage of assignments (thirty-five of eighty-five assignments, or 41 percent) was at the remembering level, which is the lowest level in the lower order. These results are summarized in figure 4.4.

| | Taxonomic Level | Number of Assignments | Percentage of Assignments |
|---|---|---|---|
| **Higher Order** | Creating | 3 | 4% |
| | Evaluating | 8 | 9% |
| | Analyzing | 8 | 9% |
| | **Total** | **19** | **22%** |
| **Lower Order** | Applying | 13 | 15% |
| | Understanding | 18 | 21% |
| | Remembering | 35 | 41% |
| | **Total** | **66** | **78%** |

Note: Because the figures are rounded to the nearest whole number, the percentages might not add to an even 100%.

Figure 4.4: Collection of student work analyzed in terms of Bloom's Revised Taxonomy of Educational Objectives.

## Alignment to State or Common Core Standards

Another kind of data to display regarding the analysis of student work is the alignment of classroom assignments to state or Common Core standards. The evaluation team members who complete this assessment must therefore be familiar with the state or Common Core standards.

In this analysis, each unique assignment is compared to grade-level standard statements to assess the match between the assignment and the grade-level expectation as described in the standard. Four ratings are possible, as shown in figure 4.5.

| Level of Achievement | Number of Assignments | Percentage of Assignments |
|---|---|---|
| Exceeded the grade-level standard | 11 | 13% |
| Met the grade-level standard | 39 | 46% |
| Below the grade-level standard | 33 | 39% |
| Could not be determined | 2 | 2% |
| **Total** | **85** | **100%** |

Figure 4.5: Alignment of student work with Common Core standards.

This example displays all student work grouped together at the school level. If you are focusing on the *vertical alignment* of assignments to the standards (the degree to which assignments are at the standard level from one grade to another), it is helpful to display these data by grade level. If the focus is on *horizontal alignment* (within a particular grade level), it is most helpful to display these data by classroom or class.

If the written curriculum in one or more subjects or grade levels is part of the selected data collection method, the team may include an analysis of the degree to which curriculum documents align to the topics and cognitive demand of state or Common Core standards. These documents may include curriculum maps, pacing charts, textbooks, supplemental programs, or intervention programs. The team analyzes the following aspects of the written curriculum's alignment (Dunsworth & Billings, 2009):

- To state or Common Core standards

- From grade to grade

- Within all classrooms at each grade level

- To textbooks and other instructional materials

- To common assessments used at each grade level

- To grade-level and schoolwide intervention and enrichment materials

Conducting a full analysis of the data and deciding on the most meaningful way to display and present that data to others will prepare your team to present that information to stakeholders. You will now be able to use the data to support conversations and make recommendations about the program going forward.

# CHAPTER 5

# Using the Results of the Program Evaluation

Once the evaluation team has completed the analysis of the data, the review moves into the final stages: reporting, recommending, and decision making. In the decision-making stage, the results of the data analysis are used to determine the performance level of the program, practice, or strategy and what, if any, actions should be taken to address performance deficits.

## Linking the Data to the Purpose for the Evaluation

Consider a program review whose purpose is to evaluate the effectiveness of an existing math program. The data analysis might show that while all students are not meeting grade-level standards, there has been a steep and steady increase over time in math scores both across grade levels and by all subgroups. On the other hand, the data analysis might show that there is less improvement than anticipated, that not all students are benefiting equally from the program, or that the school may be doing relatively well in math compared to the rest of the state but not as well as other similar schools.

The evaluation team will need to determine whether the current outcomes or results of the program, practice, or strategy are satisfactory or not, and what actions the team will recommend as a result. The results and recommendations can be classified into four groups according to whether a program, practice, or strategy has been shown to be:

1. **Highly effective.** The evaluation has shown that the program is yielding results greater than expected. The recommendation would be to continue the program as it is currently configured, and perhaps to expand the program.

2. **Effective.** The evaluation has shown that the program is yielding results equal to those expected. In this case, the recommendation would be to continue with the program, practice, or strategy as it is currently configured.

3. **Marginally effective.** The evaluation has shown that the program is yielding results that are somewhat less than those expected (or promised) when the program was implemented. In this case, the recommendation would likely be to continue with the program, practice, or strategy and (1) build in modifications or enhancements to increase its effectiveness or (2) identify a supplementary program, practice, or strategy designed to provide the desired results for a subset of the population. Given either of these decisions, the plan would need to be coupled with follow-up monitoring to ensure the results are improving with all populations.

4. **Ineffective.** The evaluation has shown that the program, despite fidelity of implementation, is yielding results that are well below those expected when the program was implemented. In this case, the recommendation will likely be to replace the program, practice, or strategy. If the program has not been implemented with fidelity, an alternative recommendation would be to re-examine the program requirements and procedures, and to re-initiate the program, ensuring that it is executed as designed.

# Using the Data for Decision Making

Once the performance level has been determined, decisions about next steps are in order. If the data analysis shows that the program is yielding results that are at the *highly effective* or *effective* levels, no modifications to the program and its implementation will be required *at this time*. In fact, the recommendation may be to extend the program to other classes or grade levels.

If the data analysis shows that the program is *marginally effective*, the team will need to determine if it will recommend modifying, strengthening, or supplementing the program. If so, it will have two tasks. The first is to make recommendations to the principal or district leadership team describing ways in which the program could be modified or supplemented to improve results. The second is to identify the data to be monitored to ensure that the program is getting back on track.

The team's thorough analysis of the data collected during the evaluation will provide the insights necessary to determine how to modify, strengthen, or supplement an existing, marginally effective program. Strategies to modify or strengthen a program include ensuring that the program is implemented with fidelity, providing for additional professional development for new and veteran staff members, or providing more time for grade-level planning. These strategies could also include modifications to the ways the program is currently configured. These recommendations could include providing additional time for students to work with the program each day, implementing grouping strategies for more individualized instruction, aligning lessons to state or Common Core standards, placing greater emphasis on tasks that require higher-order thinking, or increasing the use of formative assessments to improve instructional delivery.

If it is determined that the existing program, practice, or strategy is meeting the needs of a large percentage of the student population (80 percent or so) or it is not producing the desired results for a specific subset of students, then selecting a supplement, rather than replacing the comprehensive program, may be the best course of action. Supplemental materials that focus on a particular area or skill are then used in addition to the core program.

Supplemental materials should be considered if, for example, the team finds that students are performing well in four of the five math domains at grade 4 (operations and algebraic thinking, number and operations in base 10, number and operations—fractions, measurement and data), but are not achieving nearly as well in the fifth domain (geometry). This indicates that a supplemental program, practice, or strategy targeted directly at the geometry domain could address the identified weakness in the comprehensive program, rather than discarding it and starting with a totally new comprehensive program.

When a marginally effective program is modified or supplemented to increase its effectiveness, plans must be made to closely monitor both the modifications and the outcomes to ensure that the results are improving.

If the program is shown to be *ineffective*, fidelity should, once again, be considered. If fidelity has been ruled out as an issue, it is time to replace the program with one that is better suited to the needs of the school.

# Making Final Decisions

While it is up to the evaluation team to make the decision about the level of program effectiveness, the team usually does not make final decisions about what actions will be taken if the program, practice, or strategy is found to be marginal or ineffective. The team has invested a great deal of time in looking deeply at the data and discussing the intricacies of the program. Therefore, team members should be seen as the impartial experts, and their role is to make research-based recommendations and to support the recommendations with evidence and rationale. The recommendations should be included in the evaluation report and become part of the communication that will follow.

The decisions to modify, supplement, or discard the program, practice, or strategy are the purview of the principal, leadership council, or administrative team who will carefully review the findings and recommendations and determine what actions will be taken as a result. Usually, the evaluation team makes a presentation to the decision makers, at which time administrators or the leadership team carefully question the evaluation team about the process, data, and recommendations. Frequently, the principal will ask the evaluation team to do some additional review or analysis prior to making a final decision. The decisions will be included in the evaluation report and be communicated to staff members and other stakeholders. More about presenting the findings is included in the next chapter.

# 6

# Communicating Results

Once the collected information has been analyzed, and recommendations and decisions have been made, it is time to communicate that information to stakeholders. The findings should be communicated in such a way that multiple audiences can easily understand them. This aids in building support should any programmatic changes be called for.

## Creating the Program Evaluation Report

Every program evaluation should include a brief written report summarizing the reason for the evaluation, the research questions, the data collection and analysis, the evaluation team's recommendations, and decisions resulting from the evaluation. Consider the different audiences to whom the report will be disseminated (such as teachers, parents, and community members), and strive for an understandable tone that is not filled with jargon or acronyms so that the report conveys a clear message to all groups. The report should be succinct and present the information objectively. Figure 6.1 provides an outline of an evaluation team report.

I. Abstract highlighting key findings and recommendations

II. Purpose of the evaluation (including the research questions)

III. Participants on the evaluation team and their roles

IV. A brief description of the kinds of data collected

V. Data analysis (focused on the evaluation's purpose statement and the research questions)

VI. Answers to the research questions using the data collected

VII. Determination of the overall effectiveness of the program, practice, or strategy

VIII. Recommendations of the evaluation team

IX. Decisions

X. Next steps and timelines

Figure 6.1: Sample program evaluation report outline.

# Who Should Be Included in Communications About the Results?

The results of the program evaluation should be broadly disseminated. Many schools use the school's website for this kind of communication. In other schools, communication occurs primarily through presentations to stakeholder groups.

For example, the evaluation team and leadership team may decide to make a joint presentation to both teachers and other interested groups, such as the parent-teacher organization and the school board. Team members can highlight key points and supporting graphic displays. The presentation should be designed to encourage the audience to ask questions and offer input. Copies of the evaluation report should always be available to stakeholders.

Although you may use slightly different approaches for different audiences, the following suggestions will help ensure that both the report and the recommendations are understood and supported:

- Approach the presentation as if you were telling a story. Walk your audience through the program evaluation process, and explain what you found.

- Strive to be concise in conveying the important findings and conclusions of the evaluation.

- Don't use jargon.

- Explain technical procedures in plain English.

- Use a few key charts and graphs to help clarify the meaning of the data.

- Do not confuse the audience by providing extraneous information that does not contribute to understanding.

- Clearly state recommendations and decisions based on the results of the evaluation.

- Outline next steps that will be taken as a result of the evaluation and how they are related to the findings of the evaluation.

- Explain what those decisions will mean for the school, students, parents, and staff.

Charts and graphs go a long way in making the report and the decisions that grow from the data clear to stakeholders. Quotes can also be used. They can be powerful and add much to a report, but they should not be attributable to any one individual. They can be stated as, "One upper elementary teacher commented that . . ." or "A primary student gave this example . . ." Individuals should not be identified by name and, in the case of small groups such as counselors, not by job title.

School leaders will find that presenting the information in person generates more interest than simply making a report available on the school website, delivering it to the school board, or even sending it home. PowerPoint slides can help in organizing and displaying your findings to an audience—if done well.

# Tips for Presenting Results of the Program Evaluation

- Consider co-presenting with one or two of the evaluation team members who worked on the evaluation. This is most powerful if parents co-present to parents, teachers co-present to teachers, and so on.

- Begin by recognizing and thanking each of the evaluation team members.

- Start with data such as how many surveys were reviewed and how many interviews, observations, and focus groups were conducted. This will illustrate the depth of the evaluation.

- Keep the presentation short, leaving lots of time for discussion.

- Provide handouts with room for notes.

- Provide contact information for participants to use if they have additional questions and comments that come to mind after the presentation.

If the group is large, use group process techniques (such as think-pair-share) to ensure that everyone is able to share his or her thoughts and ideas. If the group is not too large, the comment period can be a whole-group activity. For smaller groups, one of the co-presenters can be designated to take notes and record each group's thoughts and ideas. For a large group, it works well to capture comments on poster paper so all can see that the individual ideas are being recorded.

Don't be surprised if some still resist change, even though you have involved and kept all stakeholders involved in the program evaluation. Change is seldom comfortable. Have confidence in the process—it is fair, objective, and powerful. Be ready to bring the conversation back to the data and away from anecdotal or emotional reasons for programmatic decisions.

# 7

# Looking Back and Planning Forward

While a program evaluation has a discrete beginning and end, it is only one component in an ongoing, data-driven school improvement cycle. Often the team process used in the evaluation grows to become a routine way of making research-based decisions. In this chapter, we look back on the program evaluation process and discuss strategic planning processes that should be embedded in the fabric of a high-performing school.

## Are There Other Uses for the Findings?

A well-done program evaluation will generate considerable information about the program and, perhaps more broadly, about the school. Most likely you will find many other uses for the information gathered. Consider the example in which a school's K–3 math curriculum was reviewed to determine the degree to which it readied students for grade 4. The information derived may provide important insights into the efficacy of the textbook or other instructional materials in use, the need for tighter instructional alignment between and within grade levels, the effectiveness of existing intervention and enrichment programs and materials, or the need for professional development.

## Program Evaluation as a Part of Strategic Planning

Program evaluation is an important component of strategic planning. Strategic plans are based on data that are used to focus school improvement efforts. The program evaluation process described in this guide contains many of the essential components of strategic planning. Following are some of the components of a research-based strategic planning process:

- There is a process in place, and support for, schoolwide strategic planning.
- The strategic plan is focused on student learning and refining teaching practices.

- As a part of strategic planning, student achievement and demographic data are reviewed and analyzed.

- A research-driven approach is used to identify problems and solutions.

- Extensive communication ensures that all stakeholders are a part of the decision-making process.

- An action plan describes the steps to be taken toward attainment of the goals.

- The strategic plan is put into action with fidelity.

- The school monitors progress toward attainment of goals and makes adjustments when appropriate. (Dunsworth & Billings, 2009, p. 264)

# Creating an Environment of Reflective Inquiry

In program evaluation, schools engage in "asking penetrating questions, challenging assumptions, and carefully examining the implications of their actions and choices," and in doing so, they begin to create the environment of reflective inquiry that is "a common trait of schools that are successful in maintaining improvement efforts" (McREL, n.d.). To create an environment in your school that is friendly to program evaluation, do the following:

- Work to help staff understand that the intent is to evaluate programs, not people.

- For every new initiative, determine in advance how its success will be measured and when that measurement will occur.

- Build program evaluation into the school's strategic planning process.

- Coordinate data collection procedures so that multiple evaluation questions can be answered in one data collection.

- Don't make program evaluation too much of a good thing—not every question needs to be answered through program evaluation.

- Widely share the results of the program evaluation, and refer to it frequently as decisions are made about the program, practice, or strategy studied.

- Celebrate completed evaluations by publicly recognizing those who participated in the work.

# Recognizing Effort

The first evaluation, like the first attempt at any complex endeavor, is the most difficult. Be sure to bring closure to the program evaluation by calling the evaluation team together one last time. Use this time to celebrate the accomplishment, and debrief the experience with an eye toward improving the process for the next evaluation. Ask the team to help in answering these four questions, and use the answers to help plan your next evaluation:

1.  What went well, and why?

2.  What did not go so smoothly, and why?

3.  What do you wish you had known that you didn't?

4.  What advice would you have for the next evaluation team?

# Follow-Up Program Monitoring

For the first year or two following the evaluation, it's a good idea to establish an annual mini-evaluation plan. This will ensure that the recommendations of the evaluation are implemented and garnering the hoped-for results. This can be as simple as collecting and analyzing data on a small subset of the most important variables identified in the original evaluation. The findings should be shared with staff and stakeholders and integrated into future decision making.

# Embedding Program Evaluation in the Culture of the School

A successful school evaluation process helps build a shared sense of mission and commitment among the school staff. It also may function as a way to develop increased capacity through training of the evaluation team and communication of methodology to school staff. In essence, it can become a schoolwide learning opportunity for parents, staff, and any other stakeholders involved in the process. It can help to build skills in communication, planning, problem solving, data collection, analysis and interpretation, and decision making (W. K. Kellogg Foundation, 2004).

Because program evaluation increases the quality of information on which schoolwide decisions are made, it changes both the way these decisions are made and how they are perceived. Because it involves stakeholders every step of the way, it is data-based, fair, and objective. In addition, this inclusiveness and objectivity build support for the evaluation process and an understanding of the basis upon which the decisions are reached.

As staff members become familiar with the program evaluation process, they change the way they look at and use data for themselves in their own classrooms and when making grade-level decisions. Helping your staff members develop the skills they need to routinely evaluate school programs and encouraging them in data-based decision making brings them on as partners and promotes reflective inquiry—and it gives them a stake in the outcome. While when first considered, program evaluation seems mundane, its effects on student achievement and staff morale can be culture changing. It is the responsibility of school leaders to continue asking the hard questions, evaluating practice, and providing teachers with the tools they need to accelerate student learning.

# APPENDIX

# The Vocabulary of Program Evaluation

# The Vocabulary of Program Evaluation

Program evaluation, like every field, has its own vocabulary. This vocabulary ensures that everyone working on the evaluation shares a common understanding when discussing program evaluation and its concepts and procedures. Keeping the language of program evaluation in mind as you plan for and conduct the evaluation will help keep you on track toward producing a quality product. Some of the terms may be familiar to you, while others may be new. Use this handout as a reference throughout the program evaluation process.

## Averages: Mean, Median, Mode, and Outliers

An ability to calculate *averages* is important for working with and understanding the significance of sets of data, such as that illustrated in figure A.1.

$$
\begin{array}{r}
1{,}000 \\
+1{,}000 \\
+1{,}000 \\
+1{,}000 \\
+1{,}000 \\
+2{,}000 \\
+3{,}000 \\
+3{,}000 \\
+3{,}000 \\
+3{,}000 \\
\underline{+100{,}000{,}000} \\
100{,}019{,}000
\end{array}
$$

$$100{,}019{,}000 \div 11 = 9{,}092{,}636.36$$

Figure A.1: Calculating the mean of a sample data set.

### Mean

The *mean* is what most people think of when they say *average*. To calculate the mean, add all of the numbers in a set, and then divide by the number of figures in the set. In figure A.1, there are eleven numbers in the set.

### Median

The *median* is that point above which and below which half of the group falls. In figure A.1, the median is 2,000, because half of the numbers are larger than 2,000, and half are smaller.

## Mode

The *mode* is the number that occurs most frequently in a set. In figure A.1, the mode is 1,000.

## Outliers

An *outlier* is an extremely low or high value in a set of numbers. In figure A.1, that number is 100,000,000. Including an outlier in your data set can skew the results. For example, the mean of the numbers in figure A.1 when the single 100,000,000 figure is included is 9,092,636.36. Eliminating that outlier, the calculation becomes 16,000 ÷ 10, which at 1,600 is much more representative of the range of numbers in the list. It is a good idea to determine how the group will handle outliers before beginning data collection (Bracey, 2003).

## Charts and Graphs

An easy-to-use resource for understanding strengths, differences, and how to create various data displays is the Maryland Department of Education's School Improvement in Maryland website (n.d.) (http://mdk12.org/instruction/curriculum/mathematics/math_guidelines.html).

At this site you will find guidelines and examples in creating the following displays:

- Bar graphs

- Box-and-whisker plots

- Circle graphs

- Frequency tables

- Line graphs

- Scatter plots

- Line plots

- Pictographs

- Stem-and-leaf plots

## Cognitive Demand

*Cognitive demand* (sometimes referred to as *depth of knowledge*) is the level of thinking required of a student in order to complete a given assignment. In order to provide students with the knowledge and skills necessary for them to meet a particular grade-level standard, instruction must be aimed at the level of cognitive demand specified in the standard. Similarly, in order for an assessment to result in accurate information about the progress of a student or group of students toward the standard, the cognitive demand of the assessment must match the cognitive demand of the content standard. Table A.1 provides an overview of different levels of cognitive demand as measured by Bloom's Revised Taxonomy.

Table A.1: Cognitive Demand as Measured by Bloom's Revised Taxonomy of Educational Objectives

| Higher-Order Thinking Skills | |
|---|---|
| Creating | Putting elements together to form a coherent or functional whole; reorganizing elements into a new pattern or structure through generating, planning, or producing |
| Evaluating | Making judgments based on criteria and standards through checking and critiquing |
| Analyzing | Breaking material into constituent parts, determining how the parts relate to one another and to an overall structure or purpose through differentiating, organizing, and attributing |
| Lower-Order Thinking Skills | |
| Applying | Carrying out or using a procedure through executing or implementing |
| Understanding | Constructing meaning from oral, written, and graphic messages through interpreting, exemplifying, classifying, summarizing, inferring, comparing, and explaining |
| Remembering | Retrieving, recognizing, and recalling relevant knowledge from long-term memory |

Source: Anderson & Krathwohl, 2001, pp. 67–68

## Fidelity of Implementation

*Fidelity* incorporates two concepts: "*adherence* to the intervention's core content components and *competent* execution using accomplished teaching practices" (Forgatch, Patterson, & DeGarmo, 2005, p. 3). This means that the program, practice, or strategy is fully carried out as designed by the creator or program provider. It also implies implementation by individuals experienced in the program's delivery.

Fidelity of implementation is essential to the success of a program because

> the way a program is implemented influences whether the program will be effective, or not effective. Poor implementation or lack of fidelity of implementation can, and often does, change or diminish impact. Also, once a program has been modified, no one quite knows how it will operate or what unexpected consequences it might produce. (California Department of Education, 2006, p. 1)

## Formative and Summative Program Evaluation

Just as in student evaluation, program evaluation uses two kinds of assessments: *formative* and *summative*. One of the clearest descriptions of the difference between the two is Robert Stake's analogy: "When the cook tastes the soup, that's formative; when the guest tastes it, that's summative" (as cited in Frechtling, 2002, p. 8).

As the analogy illustrates, formative assessment is used to sample the program as it exists at that moment, when time still remains to modify it. Summative assessment is used to answer questions about the impact of the program. It cannot be used to change what has already occurred, but it can be used to modify future renditions of the program.

# Generalizability

*Generalizability* is the concept behind representative sampling. It is the concept that conclusions based on the responses of a sample population can, in certain circumstances, be extended to the population as a whole. The larger the sample, the more generalizable the findings. When sample sizes are small, the less generalizable the findings. This has meaning in school-level program evaluation because sample sizes will range from large to small. For example, if the evaluation is looking at a math intervention program used in the primary grades, interviewing only one class out of three at each grade level will not give an adequate sample to be generalizable. A sample of one is simply not large enough to ensure that the findings are generalizable. However, if in a school of 300 students, 270 (90 percent) responded to a survey, it is likely that the results would be generalizable to the other students.

# Goals

*Goals* are public statements that define how good *good enough* is. These statements must include measurements that describe how the school community will know when the goal has been reached and a time frame within which the goal will be met.

# Inter-Rater Reliability

*Inter-rater reliability* refers to the consistency in scoring when more than one person is involved in that scoring. Inter-rater reliability is strong when different raters obtain the same or very close to the same scores when using an identical data collection instrument with the same individual in the same circumstances. This is a consideration when measures such as classroom or other observations are made by more than one observer. It means that all of the raters assign scores that are the same, or very close to the same, no matter who does the observation.

# Objectives

*Objectives* are checkpoints or milestones on the pathway toward meeting the goal. Objectives must be measurable and have a *reach by* date so that the school community is able to gauge progress toward the goal.

# Program Evaluation

*Program evaluation* is a systematic, organized process to provide evidence on the effectiveness and pros and cons of programs, practices, or strategies. It can be large scale—for example, evaluating all reading programs in a district or state—or small scale—such as evaluating the math program in a single school or even within a single grade level. While large-scale evaluations are most often carried out by specialists from outside the school system, small-scale evaluations are most frequently conducted by a school team led by or under the direction of the principal.

# Research Questions

*Research questions* are the questions whose answers will address the purpose of the program evaluation. These questions must be specific and measurable or observable.

# Quantitative and Qualitative Data

Data used in program evaluation fall into two broad categories:

1. **Quantitative.** These data focus on numbers and other types of information that can be measured, such as how many eighth-grade students met the National Assessment of Educational Progress standards in math.

2. **Qualitative**. These data explore that which can be observed but is not easily measurable, such as people's attitudes and beliefs.

To illustrate, consider figure A.2, which illustrates the differences between the quantitative and qualitative descriptions of a latte.

| Quantitative Description of a Latte | Qualitative Description of a Latte |
|---|---|
| Serving temperature of 150 degrees | Enticing aroma |
| Ingredients: 1.25 cups of milk, 2 tablespoons of vanilla flavored syrup, and 1.5 fluid ounce of brewed espresso | Appears light tan and frothy |
| 180 calories for 12 fluid ounce latte made with whole milk, 100 calories if made with skim milk | Comforting taste of steamed sweet milk and espresso |
| 9 grams of fat made with whole milk, 0 grams of fat if made with 2% milk | Tastes even better when syrups are added to create different flavors |
| More than 300,000 sold daily | Goes well with chocolate chip cookies |

Figure A.2: Comparison of quantitative and qualitative observations.

## Reliability

*Reliability* is the extent to which data gathering would yield the same results if the evaluation were repeated by the same people under the same conditions. For the purposes of program evaluation, this is important because the most effective way to increase reliability is to ensure that the methods used for data collection are consistent. For example, suppose one program evaluator consistently runs out of time when conducting interviews and hurries through or even skips the last three questions, while another interviewer allocates an equal amount of time to each question. It is likely that this inconsistent data collection will skew the results obtained because the respondents had unequal times within which to respond to each question.

## Subgroup Populations

One facet of program evaluation is to examine whether a particular program, practice, or strategy is effective with *all* children as a group, *and* with smaller groups of children who share common characteristics. The characteristics used to subdivide student populations include the following:

- Gender
- Grade level
- Participation in 504 plans
- Receipt of special education services
- Socioeconomic status

## Validity

This means the data collection methodology will actually measure what it is supposed to measure. For example, let's assume that a program evaluation is measuring the cognitive demand of student assignments. If the data collection consisted of comparing the assignments to the levels of Bloom's Revised Taxonomy of Educational Objectives, the measure would have validity because each assignment's level of cognitive demand would be measured according to a taxonomy of higher- and lower-order thinking skills. If, however, the data collection consisted of comparing the assignments to the teacher's lesson plans, the measure would not have validity because the data collected would describe how well the assignments matched the lesson plan, but not the degree to which the assignments called for higher-order thinking skills.

# REFERENCES AND RESOURCES

Anderson, L. W., & Krathwohl, D. R. (Eds.). (2001). *A taxonomy for learning, teaching, and assessing: A revision of Bloom's taxonomy of educational objectives.* New York: Longman.

Bernhardt, V. L. (2000). Intersections: New routes open when one type of data crosses another. *Journal of Staff Development, 21*(1), 33–36.

Bloom, B., & Krathwohl, D. R. (1956). *Taxonomy of educational objectives: The classification of educational goals, by a committee of college and university examiners.* New York: Longman.

Bracey, G. W. (2003). *Understanding education statistics: It's easier (and more important) than you think.* Arlington, VA: Educational Research Service.

California Department of Education. (2006). *Getting results fact sheet: What does getting results say about implementing programs with fidelity?* Sacramento, CA: Author.

Carr, D. (2004). *Program evaluation: Measuring the value of active aging.* Washington, DC: Partnership for Prevention.

Centers for Disease Control and Prevention, Office of the Director, Office of Strategy and Innovation. (2005). *Introduction to program evaluation for public health programs: A self-study guide.* Atlanta, GA: Author.

Centers for Disease Control and Prevention, Department of Health and Human Services (2008a, July). *Using graphs and charts to illustrate quantitative data* (Evaluation Brief No. 12). Atlanta, GA: Author.

Centers for Disease Control and Prevention, Department of Health and Human Services (2008b, December). *Data collection methods for program evaluation: Observation* (Evaluation Brief No. 16). Atlanta, GA: Author.

Century, J., Freeman, C., & Rudnick M. (2008). *A framework for measuring and accumulating knowledge about fidelity of implementation (FOI) of science instructional materials.* Accessed at http://cemse.uchicago.edu/research-and-evaluation/research/foi/narst-framework.pdf on May 24, 2011.

Cicchinelli, L. F., & Barley, Z. (1999). *Evaluating for success: Comprehensive school reform. An evaluation guide for districts and schools.* Aurora, CO: Mid-continent Research for Education and Learning.

Cook, D. (2010). *Twelve tips for evaluating educational programs.* Rochester, MN: Mayo Clinic College of Medicine.

Dunsworth, M., & Billings, D. (2009). *The high-performing school: Benchmarking the 10 indicators of effectiveness.* Bloomington, IN: Solution Tree Press.

Forgatch, M. S., Patterson, G. R., & DeGarmo, D. S. (2005). *Evaluating fidelity: Predictive validity for a measure of competent adherence to the Oregon model of parent management training.* Eugene, OR: Oregon Social Learning Center.

Frechtling, J. (2002). *The 2002 user friendly handbook for project evaluation.* Arlington, VA: The National Science Foundation, Directorate for Education & Human Resources, Division of Research, Evaluation, and Communication.

Maryland Department of Education. (n.d.). Mathematics/instructional strategies: Guidelines for creating data displays. Accessed at http://mdk12.org/instruction/curriculum/math/math_guidelines.html on September 7, 2010.

McNamara, C. (n.d.). Basic guide to program evaluation. Accessed at http://managementhelp.org/evaluatn/fnl_eval.htm on October 8, 2010.

Mid-continent Research for Education and Learning. (2000). *Leadership folio series: Guiding comprehensive school reform.* Aurora, CO: Author.

Mid-continent Research for Education and Learning. (n.d.). Asking the right questions: A school change toolkit, reflective inquiry. Accessed at www.mcrel.org/toolkit/res/reflect.asp on January 4, 2011.

New York State Teacher Centers. (2008). Program evaluation. Accessed at www.programevaluation.org/focusgroups.htm on September 14, 2010.

O'Connell, J. (2007). *What does getting results say about implementing programs with fidelity? Getting results fact sheet.* Sacramento, CA: California Department of Education.

Paulsen, C. A., & Dailey, D. (2002). *Answering the question . . . What are some guidelines that I can use to evaluate my program or intervention?* Washington, DC: Elementary and Middle Schools Technical Assistance Center.

Rennekamp, R. A., & Nall, M. A. (n.d.). *Using focus groups in program development and evaluation.* Lexington: University of Kentucky. Accessed at www.ca.uky.edu/Agpsd/focus.pdf on September 9, 2010.

W. K. Kellogg Foundation. (2004). *Evaluation handbook.* Battle Creek, MI: Author.

# INDEX

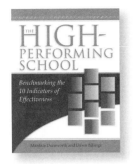

### The High-Performing School: Benchmarking the 10 Indicators of Effectiveness
*Mardale Dunsworth and Dawn Billings*
Learn the improvement process used by many schools to become high-performing schools. This book is a guide to the on-site school review—a cooperative venture between an external review team and a school's administrators, teachers, and students. **BKF294**

### Communicating and Connecting With Social Media
*William M. Ferriter, Jason T. Ramsden, and Eric C. Sheninger*
Social media holds great potential benefits for schools reaching out to our communities, preparing our teachers, and connecting with our kids. In this short text, the authors examine how enterprising schools are using social media tools to provide customized professional development for teachers and to transform communication practices with staff, students, parents, and other stakeholders. **BKF474**

### Mobile Learning Devices
*Kipp D. Rogers*
This brief guide explains why mobile learning is transforming education and how devices such as cell phones can enhance learning in 21st century classrooms. The author provides guidelines principals can use to help staff introduce mobile learning devices into instruction in ways that are safe, engaging, aligned with National Educational Technology Standards, and targeted to promote student learning. **BKF445**

### What Effective Schools Do: Re-Envisioning the Correlates
*Lawrence W. Lezotte and Kathleen McKee Snyder*
This guide helps educators implement a continuous school improvement system through application of the seven correlates of effective schools. The authors discuss each correlate, update the knowledge base, and incorporate practical ideas from practitioners in the field. A comprehensive description of practices enables educators to build and sustain a school culture that accommodates the learning expectations and needs of all students. **BKF336**

### Turning Your School Around: A Self-Guided Audit for School Improvement
*Robert D. Barr and Debra L. Yates*
Learn a step-by-step protocol for the self-guided audit that focuses on the most crucial areas of school improvement. The authors give readers a realistic view of the work involved in a top-to-bottom audit, while providing supporting evidence of its effectiveness. **BKF295**

## Solution Tree | Press

*a division of*
Solution Tree
Visit solution-tree.com or call 800.733.6786 to order.

# Solution Tree

Solution Tree's mission is to advance the work of our authors. By working with the best researchers and educators worldwide, we strive to be the premier provider of innovative publishing, in-demand events, and inspired professional development designed to transform education to ensure that all students learn.

The mission of the National Association of Elementary School Principals is to lead in the advocacy and support for elementary and middle level principals and other education leaders in their commitment for all children.